Vorwort / Foreword

Wie gelingt es, Menschen in Arbeitssitzungen und/oder Lernumgebungen zu aktivieren? Was erleichtert die Kommunikation in schwierigen Phasen? Wie kann man Dialoge und Ergebnisse so festhalten, dass man noch Jahre später mit einem Blick im Bilde ist? Wie gestaltet man aus einem Blatt Papier ein Plakat mit Aufmerksamkeitswert? Wie sieht die Alternative zu Powerpoint aus? Viele Fragen, auf die wir eine Antwort haben: Visualisierung!

Der erste bikablo® ermöglichte einen schnellen Einstieg in die Welt des »Visual Facilitating«. bikablo® 2.0 lässt nun keine Wünsche mehr offen: Sie finden hier noch mehr und vor allem speziellere Bilder und Plakatvorlagen für viele Themen rund um Personal/Persönlichkeit, Organisation, Strategie, Projektmanagement, Markt und Wirtschaft.

Hier ist nun nahezu alles drin, was in Meetings, Trainings und wann immer Menschen miteinander sprechen, planen oder lernen, zum Thema wird.

Viel Spaß beim Visualisieren!

Holger Scholz & Martin Haussmann
bikablo® akademie

Guido Neuland
Neuland GmbH & Co.KG

P.S.: Wir haben uns entschieden, den »Männchen« in unserem Vokabular Lebewohl zu sagen und sprechen künftig von »Figuren«. Wegen der besseren Lesbarkeit verzichten wir im Text auf die gleichzeitige Verwendung weiblicher und männlicher Personenbegriffe. Gemeint und angesprochen sind natürlich immer beide Geschlechter :-)

How is it possible to activate people in work sessions and/or learning environments? What makes communication effective at difficult stages? How can one record dialogue and results so clearly that you know exactly what has happened at a glance even years later? How can you turn a piece of paper into powerful attention-grabbing poster? What is the alternative to PowerPoint? We have one answer to all these questions: Visualization!

The first bikablo® was a quick introduction to the world of 'Visual Facilitating'. This version, bikablo® 2.0, leaves nothing to be desired: You will find even more specialised pictures and poster templates for all sorts of issues relating to personnel, individual personality, organisation development, strategic planning, project management, marketing and the general economy.

We hope we have covered virtually everything you could need in meetings, training sessions and anytime people come together to talk, plan or learn.

We hope you enjoy visualizing!

Holger Scholz & Martin Haussmann
bikablo® akademie

Guido Neuland,
Neuland GmbH & Co.KG

p.s.: We have decided to bid farewell to the 'manikin' in our terminology and will from now on talk about 'figures'. Also, to make the text easier to read, we will not use male and female language. Of course, we are always speaking about both sexes :-)

Inhaltsverzeichnis / Table of Contents

Vorwort 2
Inhaltsverzeichnis 3
Schlagwortverzeichnis 5
Insider-Tipps 8

A Die wichtigsten Zutaten für Visual Facilitating 11

A1 Textcontainer 12
Banderolen, Rahmen, Gegenstände und verschiedene Formen für Überschriften und wichtige Texte

A2 Symbole 18
Zusammenstellung der bewährtesten Symbole aus der Praxis

A3 Figuren 27
Platzhalter für Einzelpersonen, Teams und Gruppen in verschiedenen Situationen, in Ruhe und Bewegung

A4 Layouts für Flipchart und Pinwand 34
Vorlagen für Flipcharts und Pinwandplakate aus der Praxis für die Praxis: Präsentationsplakate, Gruppenarbeitsplakate, Plakate für Prozessplanung und Projektmanagement u.v.m.

B Workshop, Meeting, Seminar und Training 46

B1 Prinzipien und Spielregeln 47
Visualisierungen von Prinzipien, Spielregeln und Leitgedanken für Facilitation, Beratung, Training und Themen der Organisationsentwicklung

B2 Methoden und Techniken 65
Logos und Piktogramme für viele bekannte Methoden und Techniken

B3 Seminare und Konferenzen 72
Bildvorlagen für die häufigsten Themen und Begriffe, die einem bei der Planung, Organisation und Durchführung von Seminaren und Konferenzen begegnen

---

Introduction 2
Table of contents 3
Index of keywords 5
Insider tips 8

A The most important ingredients for Visual Facilitating 11

A1 Text borders 12
Banners, frames, objects and different styles for headlines / important texts

A2 Symbols 18
Summary of the most established symbols from visualization practice

A3 Figures 27
Placeholders for individual people, teams and groups in different situations, at rest and in motion

A4 Layouts for flip charts and pin boards 34
Templates for flip charts and pin board posters from the field for the field: presentation posters, group work posters, posters for process planning and project management, and much more

B Workshops, meetings, seminars and training courses 46

B1 Principles and rules 47
Visualization of principles, rules and central themes for facilitation, consultancy, training and aspects of organisational development

B2 Methods and techniques 65
Logos and pictograms for many known methods / techniques

B3 Seminars and conferences 72
Image templates for the most frequent themes and terms you come across in the planning, organisation and execution of seminars and conferences

Inhaltsverzeichnis
Table of Contents

C Persönlichkeit, Team und Projekte 80

- **C1 persönliche Entwicklung** 81
  Hier geht es vor allem um persönliche Stärken, Herausforderungen, besondere Fähigkeiten und Entwicklungspotentiale
- **C2 Teamarbeit und Führung** 91
  Bildvorlagen für Anlässe und Veranstaltungen, in denen es um Kommunikation, Teamdynamik, Führung und Zusammenarbeit geht
- **C3 Projekte managen** 99
  Eine Bilderdatenbank rund um Begriffe und Spezialthemen für Projekte und Projektmanagement
- **C2 Informationstechnologie** 104
  Visualisierungen und piktogramm-ähnliche Zeichen rund um die Welt der Hard- und Software, Datenbanken und Netzwerke

D Unternehmen und Markt 108

- **D1 Unternehmen/Organisation** 109
  Bilder für einzelne Abteilungen, Bereiche, Standorte, Marken und Produkte
- **D2 Strategie, Kunde und Markt** 115
  Komplexere Bilder, die durch die Kombination verschiedener Symbole zum Teil sehr konkrete Bilder zum Themenfeld Strategie, Kunde und Markt enthalten

Anhang 125
- Literatur-Tipps 126
- Web-Tipp 127
- Produkte 128
- Fortbildungen der bikablo® akademie 134
- Die Autoren, Impressum 135

C Personality, team and projects 80

- **C1 Personal development** 81
  Here, the main emphasis is on personal strengths, challenges, special skills and potential for development
- **C2 Teamwork and leadership** 91
  Image templates for occasions and events relating to communication, team dynamics, leadership and cooperation.
- **C3 Managing projects** 99
  An image database with terms and special issues for projects and project management
- **C2 Information technology** 104
  Visualizations and pictogram-like symbols relating to the world of hardware and software, databases and networks

D Company and market 108

- **D1 Company/Organisation** 109
  Pictures for individual departments, areas, sites, brands and products
- **D2 Strategy, customer and market** 115
  More complex pictures combining different symbols to become concrete images on strategy, the customer and the market

Appendix 125
- Literature recommendations 126
- Web recommendations 127
- Products 128
- bikablo® akademie further trainings 134
- The authors, credits 135

Schlagwortverzeichnis – Key Word Index

360 Grad-Feedback 69 ›››A››› Abendprogramm 79 · abgeschlossenes Projekt 100 · Ablehnung 94 · Abreise 76 · Abschwung 123 · Abteilung 110 · Administration 113, 120 · Administrator 107 · Agenda 35 · Aggression 90 · Akquisition 117 · Angel · Angriff 82 · Angst loswerden 83 · Angst zulassen 83 · Anker · Annahmen 48 · Anreise 76 · Ansage 95 · Anteilseigner 110 · Apfel 25 · Apfelbaum 20 · Appreciative Inquiry 40, 54, 66 · Assessment 69 · Aufschwung 123 · Aufsichtsrat 110 · Aufstellung 70 · Aufstieg 97 · Auftrieb 98 · Auge 21 · Augenhöhe 96 · Ausbeutung 87 · Ausdauer 88 · Ausgeglichenheit 88 · Ausgrenzung 94 · Aussage 62 · Außendienst 113 · Auswertung 69 · Auszeichnung 78 · Auto 20 ›››B››› Bahn 75 · Balance 88, 89 · Ballast 98 · Band 79 · Banderole 13 · Bank 123 · Banner 15 · Bargespräche 79 · Baum 20, 39 · Beamer 93 · Befürchtungen 93 · Benchmarking 121 · beobachten 49 · Beobachtung 54 · Bereich 110 · bereichsübergreifend 93 · Berge 96 · Beruflicher Aufstieg 82 · Besprechung 73 · Beste 54 · Betrieb 110 · Betriebsrat 111 · Betriebssystem 106 · Biene 26 · Blitzpräsentation 68 · Bombe 24 · Börse 123 · Börsenboom 123 · Börsencrash 123 · Brainstorming 67 · Briefbogen 13 · Brille 21 · Buch 14 · Budgetmanagement 101 · Budgetmanager 101 · Buffet 76 · Bug (Programmierfehler) 107 · Bürogebäude 20 · Bus 75 · Business Lunch 76 · Businesstheater 78 ›››C››› Callcenter 113 · Cash Cow 117 · Change 116 · Change Management 111 · Check-in 74 · Come Together 79 · Community Building 64 · Controlling 112 · Cultural Diversity 122 ›››D››› Datei 107 · Datenbank 106 · Defensive 82 · Deliverables 103 · demografischer Wandel 124 · Denkweise 48 · Dialog 48 · Dialog 93 · Differenzen 59 · Direktvertrieb 114 · Diversität 94 · Dokument 106 · Dokumentation 73, 103 · Dreamteam 98 · Dresscode (casual · business casual · business · gala) 79 · Drucker 105 · Dusche 15 ›››E››› EDV-Training 71 · Ehrung 78 · Eigenliebe 82 · Eignungstest 69 · eine Sprache sprechen 92 · einfache Sprache benutzen 92 · Einheitsgröße 121 · Einkauf 111 · Eisberg 39 · Elefant 51 · Elektrik 23 · E-Mail 106 · Empfang 76, 78 · Endkunde 118 · Energizer 69 · Entscheidung 95 · Entscheidungsmut 95 · Entschlossenheit 89 · Entwicklung 124 · Erfahrungen (berichten) 61 · Erfolg 97 · Erfolge messen 121 · Ergebnispräsentation 68 · Ergebnisse 103 · Erkundender 48 · EU-Staaten 124 · Evaluation 69 · Explosion 24 · Externe Trends 41 ›››F››› Fabrik 20 · Facilitation, Facilitator 50, 60 · Facility-Management 113 · Fähigkeiten entecken 83 · Fahne 15 · Fallschirm 24 · Familienaufstellung 70 · Feedback 69, 98 · Feedbacksammlung 37 · Fehler-Report 107 · Fehlersuche 107 · Feuer 24 · Feuerlöscher 25 · Finanzen 112 · Finanzielle Absicherung 84 · Finanzkrise 123 · Fingerfood 76 · Firmenkulturen 122 · Firmenumzug 117 · Fish Bowl 67 · Fläche 120 · Fleiß 98 · Flexibilität 88 · Flipchartmarker 23 · Flugzeug 20, 75 · Fokus 56, 59 · Forschung und Entwicklung 112 · Forum 77 · Frage 51, 55, 95 · FTP-Zugang 106 · Führen 97 · Führung 95 · Fusion 117, 122 ›››G››› Gala-Dinner 79 · Galashow 79 · Galerie 67 · Garderobe 76 · Gastredner 77 · Gebäude-Management 113 · Gedanken 93 · Gegenwind 82 · Gehirn 21 · Gelassenheit 88 · Geld 20, 120 · Geldscheine 20 · Gemeinsamkeiten 58 · Gemeinschaft 64 · Generalist 87 · Gesamtprozess 97 · Geschäftserfolg 122 · Geschäftsführung 110 · Geschäftskunde 118 · Geschäfts-Möglichkeit 119 · Gesetz der zwei Füße 52 · Gewitterwolke 16 · Giesskanne 22 · Glad · Sad · Mad 40 · global denken, lokal handeln 122 · Globales Portfolio 116 · Globalisierung 124 · Glocke 25 · Glühbirne 19 · Gruppe 60 · Gruppenarbeit 59 · Gruppencoaching 98

360 degree Feedback 69 ›››A››› A la carte menu 79 · Accuracy 90 · Acquisition 117 · Acquisition 118 · Across departments 93 · Administration 113, 120 · Administration work 120 · Administrator 107 · Advertising 111 · Aeroplane 20, 75 · Agenda 35 · Aggression 90 · Aid package 24 · Alarm clock 24 · Anchor 22 · Announcement 95 · Apple 25 · Apple tree 20 · Appreciative Inquiry 40, 54, 66 · Arrival 76 · Arrow 17 · Aspects of character 86 · Assessment 69 · Assumptions 48 · Attack 82 · Award 78 ›››B››› Background 100 · Balance 88, 89 · Band 79 · Bank 123 · Bank notes 20 · Banner 13, 15 · Bar meetings 79 · Bees 26 · Behaviour training 71 · Bell 25 · Benchmarking 121 · Best 54 · Biscuits 76 · Black sheep 94 · Board 110 · Bomb 24 · Book 14 · Box 15 · Brain 21 · Brainstorming 67 · Branches 114 · Brand 114 · Break 60, 76 · Budget management 101 · Budget manager 101 · Buffet 76 · Bug (programming error) 107 · Building Management 113 · Bumble bee 26, 53 · Bus 75 · Business Lunch 76 · Business opportunity 119 · Business success 122 · Business theatre 78 · Business to Business 118 · Business to Customer 118 · Butterflies 53 ›››C››› Calendar 23 · Call centre 113 · Calm 88 · Campfire 24 · Candle 25 · Capabilities 83, 86 · Car 20 · Car park 75 · Career 82 · Cash Cow 117 · Celebration 78 · Change 51, 116 · Change Management 111 · Change of site 117 · Check-in 74 · Cloakroom 76 · Cloud 16 · Clover leaf 26 · Coffee 76 · Coffee break 53, 60 · Coins 20 · Collection of feedback 37 · Collection of ideas 37 · Collection of themes 36 · Communication training 71 · Community 64 · Community Building 64 · Company 110 · Company culture 122 · Company relocation 117 · Company success 98 · Compass 19 · Competition 119 · Completed project 100 · Composure 88 · Computer 105 · Computer centre 105 · Concentration 89 · Condition 88 · Conference paperwork 73 · Conflicts 58 · Connect 57 · Conscientiousness 98 · Consensus 58 · Constellation 70 · Control group 73 · Controlling 112 · Cooperation 98 · Coordination 90 · Corporate communication 113 · Cosy chat 78 · Courage 89, 95 · Creative workshop 70 · Crown 20 · Cultural Diversity 122 · Cup 19, 23 · Customer 118 · Cycle 17 ›››D››› Dance 79 · Data Centre 105 · Database 106 · Decision 95 · Decisiveness 89 · Defence 82 · Defensive 82 · Deliverables 103 · Demographic change 124 · Department 110 · Departure 76 · Description 13 · Development 124 · Dialogue 48, 93 · Difference(s) 55, 59, 94 · Direct sales 114 · Distribution 111 · Diver 39 · Diversity 94, 122 · Division 110 · Document 106 · Documentation 73, 103 · Doorbell 25 · Downturn 123 · Dream team 98 · Dresscode (casual · business casual · business · gala) 79 ›››E››› Ear 21 · Economic crisis 124 · Economic trend 123 · Electrics 23 · Elements of personality 86 · Elephant 51 · E-mail 106 · Energizer 69 · Error report 107 · EU countries 124 · Evaluation 69 · Evening programme 79 · Exclusion 94 · Experiences 61 · Exploitation 87 · Explorer 48 · Explosion 24 · Express clearly 63 · External sales 113 · External trends 41 · Eye 21 · Eye-level 96 ›››F››› Facilitation, Facilitator 50, 60, 73 · Facility Management 113 · Factory 20 · Family listing 70 · Fear 83, 93 · Feedback 69, 98 · File 107 · Finances 112 · Financial crisis 123 · Financial security 84 · Finger food 76 · Fire 24 · Fire extinguisher 25 · Fish Bowl 67 · Fishing rod 24 · Flag 15 · Flexibility 88 · Flip chart marker 23 · Focus 56, 59 · Folder 25 · Forum 77 · Fruit 76 · FTP access 106 · Fun 57 · Funnel 25 · Fusion 117, 122 · Future 54, 59 · Future Search 41, 58, 66 · Future Workshop 60, 66 ›››G››› Gala dinner 79 · Gala show 79 · Gallery 67 · Generalist 87 · Get together 79

Schlagwortverzeichnis·
Key Word Index

>>>H>>> Haifisch 22 · Hammer 21 · Hand 21 · Handout 73 · Handy 23 · Hängematte 26 · Herz 19, 56 · Hierarchie-Ebene 95 · Hilfspaket 24 · Hintergrund 100 · Hirn 21 · Hochhaus 20 · Hören 56 · Hostessen 74 · Hummeln 26, 153 · >>>I>>> ICE 75 · Ich-Aussagen 64 · Ideenmanagement 122 · Ideensammlung 37 · Identität 122 · Implementierung 116 · Improvisationstheater 78 · Impulsvortrag 77 · In Scope 44, 103 · Inflation 123 · Infomarkt 42 · Infomarkt 67 · Information 100 · Informationsfluss 100 · Informationsflut 97 · Informationsschalter 74 · Informationstausch 100 · Informationstransfer 93 · informiert werden 92 · Inhaber 110 · Innendienst 113 · Integration 94 · Internationales Business 122 · Internationalisierung 124 · Interne Kommunikation 112 · interner Kunde 118 · Internet 106 · Interview 68 · Intuition 82 · IT 111 · >>>J>>> Jubiläum 78 · >>>K>>> Kaffee 76 · Kaffeepause 53 · Kalender 23 · Kamingespräch 78 · Karriere 82 · Karteikarten 14 · Kerze 25 · Killerphrasen 62 · Kiste 15 · klar(e Sprache) 63 · Klartext reden 92 · Kleeblatt 26 · Kleiderbügel 23 · Kleingruppenarbeit 68 · Klingel 25 · Kommunikationstraining 71 · Kompass 19 · Kompetenzen 86 · Kondition 88 · Konflikt 58 · König 118 · Konjunktur 123 · Konsens 58 · Konzentration 89 · Kooperation 98 · Koordination 90 · Kraft 89 · Kraft des Zuhörens 49 · Kreativ-Werkstatt 70 · Krone 20 · Kunde 118 · Kundengewinnung 118 · >>>L>>> Lager 113 · Lagerfeuer 24 · Laptop 105 · Lautsprecher 25 · Leidenschaft 97 · Lernbereitschaft 85 · Lernender 48 · Lernschritte 36, 85 · Lernstufen 85 · Leuchtturm 22 · Leute mitnehmen 95 · Licht 74 · Lieferanten 114 · Lineal 23 · Logistik 112 · Lösungsvorschlag 96 · Lupe 19 · >>>M>>> Magnet 26 · Mappe 25 · Marke 114 · Marker 23 · Marketing 111 · Marktanalyse 119 · Marktbeobachtung 119 · Maßnahmen 63 · Mauer 97 · Meeting 73 · Meilenstein 102, 121 · Meinung 59 · Menue à la Carte 79 · Merger 117 · Mikrofon 74 · Mindmapping 37, 67 · miteinander reden 92 · Mobbing 94 · Mobilität 84 · Moderation 50, 73 · Moderator 60, 73 · Motivation 87 · Motivierung 87 · Multi-Tasking-Fähigkeit 84 · Mund 21 · Münzen 20 · Musik 79 · Muster aufbrechen 120 · Mut 89 · >>>N>>> Nachhaltigkeit 124 · Namensschild 74 · Naturerfahrung 70 · Negatives 61 · Netzwerk 105 · Netzwerktechniker 107 · Niederlassungen 114 · >>>O>>> Oberfläche 121 · Obst 76 · offen sein 48 · Offenes Forum 41 · Offenheit 85 · Offensive 82 · Offshoring 117 · Ohr 21 · Open Space 43, 52, 66 · Organisation 55 · Organisationsaufstellung 70 · Organisationsentwicklung 111 · Orgateam 73 · Out of Scope 44, 103 · Outdoor 70 · >>>P>>> Papierrolle 14 · Parkplatz 75 · Party 79 · Passwort 107 · Pause 60, 76 · PC 105 · Performance 85 · Personal 112 · Personal Computer 105 · Personalentwicklung 112 · persönliches Gespräch 93 · Persönlichkeitsanteile 86 · Perspektive 48 · Pfeil 17 · Phantasiereise 67 · Pilotgruppe 73 · Pkw 20 · Plakathalter 16 · Plan B 103 · planen 63 · Plätzchen 76 · Plenum 77 · Podiumsdiskussion 77 · Pokal 19 · Portfolio 114 · positive/negative Anteile 86 · Positives 62 · Potentiale 82 · Power 88 · Präsentation 77 · präsentieren 93 · Präzision 90 · Problem 119 · Produkt 114 · Produktion 110 · Produktionsoptimierung 120 · Produkt-Training 71 · Projekt 44, 45, 100 · Projektbeschreibung 100 · Projektion 74 · Projektlebenszyklus 101 · Projektmanagement 100, 101 · Projektmanagement-Standards 101 · Projektmanager 101 · Projektplanung 100 · Projekt-Status 101 · Protokoll 73, 107 · Prozessberatung 50 · Prozessoptimierung 120 · Public Relations 111 · Puzzle 15 · >>>Q>>> Qualitätsmanagement 112 · Qualitätssiegel 19 · >>>R>>> rausholen 119 · Reaktionsvermögen 90 · Realität 54,

Getting more out of sth. 119 · Glad · Sad · Mad 40 · Glasses 21 · global 122 · Global portfolio 116 · Globalisation 124 · Group 60 · Group coaching 98 · Group work 68 · Guardian angel 82 · Guest speaker 77 · >>>H>>> Hammer 21 · Hammock 26 · Hand 21 · Handout 73 · Hanger 23 · Harmony 88 · Head office 114, 120 · Head wind 82 · Heart 19, 56 · Honour 78 · Hostesses 74 · >>>I>>> ICE 75 · Iceberg 39 · Ideas management 122 · Identity 122 · Impetus 98 · Implementation 116 · Implementing strategies 116 · Improvisational theatre 78 · In Scope 44, 103 · Independent 58 · In-depth 57 · Index cards 14 · Inflation 123 · Info market 42, 67 · Information 100 · Information desk 74 · Information exchange 100 · Information flood 97 · Information flow 100 · Information transfer 93 · informed 92 · Insurance 84 · Integration 94 · Interaction 120 · Interfaces 103, 120 · Internal communication 112 · Internal customer 118 · Internal sales 113 · International business 122 · Internationalisation 124 · Internet 106 · Interview 68 · Intuition 82 · Involve people 95 · I statements 64 · IT 111 · IT training 71 · >>>K>>> Key 24 · Kick-off 121 · Killer phrases 62 · King 118 · Knowledge in the system 50 · >>>L>>> Language 55 · Laptop 105 · Law 112 · Law of two feet 53 · Leadership 95 · Leading 97 · Learner 48 · Learning stages 36, 85 · Learning steps 85 · Level 95 · Light bulb 19 · Lighthouse 22 · Lighting 74 · Lightning presentation 68 · Listen 56 · Listening 49 · Listing 70 · Locations 114 · Lock 24 · Logistics 112 · Loudspeaker 25 · Lower levels 120 · >>>M>>> Magnet 26 · Magnifying glass 19 · Management 110 · Marker 23 · Market analysis 119 · Market observation 119 · Marketing 111 · Measures 63 · Measuring success 121 · Meeting 73 · Merger 117 · Microphone 74 · Milestone 102, 121 · Mind 21 · Mind mapping 37, 67 · Mirror 98 · Mobbing 94 · Mobile 23 · Mobility 84 · Moderator · Moderation 50, 60, 73 · Money 20, 120 · Motivation 87 · Motivational talk 77 · Mountains 96 · Mouth 21 · Moving up 97 · Multitasking skills 84 · Music 79 · >>>N>>> Name badge 74 · Nature experience 70 · Negative 61 · Network 105 · Network technician 107 · Networking 117 · Notepaper 13 · >>>O>>> Objective(s) 63, 96 · Observation 54 · Observe 49 · Offensive 82 · Office building, high-rise 20 · Offshoring 117 · One size fits all 121 · Open forum 41 · Open Space 43, 52, 66 · Open to the floor 77 · Openly 48 · Openness 85 · Operating system 106 · Opinions 59 · Organisation 55 · Organisation list/constellation 70 · Organisational development 111 · Organisational team 73 · Out of Scope 44, 103 · Outdoor 70 · Overtime 84 · Owner 110 · >>>P>>> Padlock 24 · Pain threshold 90 · Paper roll 14 · Parachute 24 · Party 79 · Passion 97 · Password 107 · Pattern 120 · PC 105 · Performance 85 · Periscope 22 · Personal Computer 105 · Personal conversation 93 · Personnel 112 · Personnel development 112 · Perspective 48, 56 · Pilot group 73 · Plan 63 · Plan B 103 · Plan of attack 116 · Podium discussion 77 · Portfolio 114 · Positive things 62 · Positive/negative aspects 86 · Poster holder 16 · Potential 82 · Power 88, 89 · Power of listening 49 · Precision 90 · Prejudices 93 · Present 93 · Presentation 68, 77 · Printer 105 · Private view 67 · Problem 119 · Process as a whole 97 · Process Consultancy 50 · Process optimisation 120 · Product 114 · Product training 71 · Production 110 · Production optimisation 120 · Professional advancement 82 · Project 44, 45, 100 · Project description 100 · Project lifecycle 101 · Project management 100, 101 · Project management standards 101 · Project manager 101 · Project planning 100 · Project status 101 · Projecting 74 · Projector 93 · Protocol 73, 107 · Proud & Sorry 41

Schlagwortverzeichnis
Key Word Index

63 Rechenzentrum 105 · Rechner 105 · Recht 112 · Reengineering 116 · Reflexion 86 · Regenschirm 22 · Regenwolke 16 · Regionaler Markt 119 · Registrierung 74 · Restriktionen 103 · Review 69 · Rhetorik 96 · Risiko 102 · Risikobereitschaft 88 · Roadmap 38 · Roll out 116 · Roter Teppich 76 · Rückblick 78 · Rückmeldung 69 · Rucksack 22 · Ruhe 88 ›››**S**››› Sandwich-Figur 16 · S-Bahn 75 · Schädel · Schild 15, 26 · Schirm 22 · Schlachtplan 116 · Schloss 24 · Schlüssel 24 · Schmerztoleranz 90 · Schmetterlinge 53 · Schnelligkeit 89 · Schnittstellen 103, 120 · Schreibwerkstatt 70 · Schutzengel 82 · Schutzschild 26 · schwarzes Schaf 94 · Schwert 26 · Seerohr 22 · Sekretariat 113 · Selbst-Ausbeutung 87 · Selbstausdruck 85 · Selbstbewusstsein 88 · Selbstbild 86 · Selbsteinschätzung 85 · Selbstkontrolle 88 · Selbstmotivation 87 · Selbstreflexion 86 · selbststeuernd 58 · Seminar 71 · Server 105 · Service-Point 74 · Servicequalität 119 · Shuttle 75 · Sichtweise 49, 56 · Siegel 19 · Sinne 21 · Software 106 · Software-Entwicklung 106 · Sound 74 · Spaß haben 57 · Spezialist 87 · Spiegel 98 · Spielregeln 35 · Sprache 55 · Sprechblase 16 · Sprungbrett 26 · Standorte 114 · Standortverlegung 117 · Startphase 121 · Steckbrief 13 · Stecker 23 · Steuerungsgruppe 73 · Stolz & Bedauern 41 · Storytelling 40, 66 · Strang ziehen 116 · Strategie 111, 116 · Strategien umsetzen 116 · Strukturen 120 · Subventionen 124 · Supply Chain Management 113 · SWOT 43 · Symbole 18 · System 58 · Systemische Strukturaufstellung 70 ›››**T**››› Tagungsunterlagen 73 · Tanz 79 · Tasse 23 · Taucher 39 · Taxi 75 · Team 94, 97 · Teamarbeit 68 · Teambuilding 68 · Teamcoaching 98 · Teamentwicklung 68 · Teamerfolg 98 · Teamplay 90 · Technik 74 · Tee 23, 76 · Telefon 23 · Telefontraining 71 · Telefonzentrale 113 · Themensammlung 36 · Thermometer 19 · tiefergehend 57 · Timing 102 · Tischdecke 57 · Toiletten 74 · Toleranz 94 · Totenkopf 26 · Training 71 · Transfer 75 · Transport 112 · Trichter 57 · T-Shirt 23 · tun, was man sagt 92 ›››**U**››› über den Tellerrand schauen 85 · Überstunden 84 · U-Boot 22 · Uhr 24 · Umstrukturierung 116 · Unternehmen 110 · Unternehmenserfolg 98 · Unternehmenskommunikation 113 · Unterschiede 55 · Unterschiedlichkeit 94 · User 107 ›››**V**››› Verbinden 57 · Verhaltenstraining 71 · Verkauf 111 · Verkaufstraining 71 · Vernetzung 117 · Vernissage 67 · Versand 113 · Versicherung 84 · Verteidigung 82 · Vertrieb 111 · Verwaltungs-Aufgaben 120 · Vielfalt 122 · Vierraum-Wohnung 51 · Visionen 95, 96 · visualisieren 60 · Visualisierung 67 · Vorhängeschloss · Vorschlagswesen 122 · Vorstand 110 · Vortrag 77 · Vorurteile 193 ›››**W**››› Waage 19 · Wandkalender 23 · WC 74 · Wecker 24 · Wegweiser 17 · Wellenpfeil 17 · weltweit 122 · wer macht was bis wann 36 · Werbung 111 · Werkzeuge 121 · Werte 96 · Wesensteile 86 · Wettbewerb 119 · Wildnistraining 70 · Willkommensplakat 35 · Win-Win Situation 117 · Wirtschaftskrise 124 · Wissen im System 50 · WLAN 105 · Wolke 16 · Work-Life-Balance 84 · Workshop 71 · World Café 42 · World Café 56, 66 · World Wide Web 106 · Wrap-Up 78 ›››**Z**››› Zeit 60 · Zeitintervalle 60 · Zeitmanagement 101 · Zeitmanager 101 · Zentrale 114, 120 · Ziel(e) 63, 96, 102 · Zielgenauigkeit 90 · Zollstock 23 · Zuhören 49 · Zukunft 54, 59 · Zukunftskonferenz 41, 58, 67 · Zukunftswerkstatt 60, 66 · Zulieferer 114 · Zusammenfassung 78 · Zusammenspiel 120 · Zuständigkeiten 120 · Zyklus 17

Providers 114 · Public relations 111 · Pulling together 116 · Purchasing 111 · Puzzle 15 ›››**Q**››› Quality Management 112 · Quality seal 19 · Question 51, 55, 95 ›››**R**››› Rain cloud 16 · Reaction speed 90 · Reality 54, 63 · Reception 76, 78 · Red carpet 76 · Reengineering 116 · Reflection 86 · Regional market 119 · Registration 74 · Rejection 94 · Research and development 112 · Responsibilities 120 · Restrictions 103 · Restructuring 116 · Results 103 · Review 69, 78 · Rhetoric 96 · Risk 102 · Roadmap 38 · Rollout 116 · Rooms of Change 51 · Rucksack 22 · Ruler, folding rule 23 · Rules 35 ›››**S**››› Safety sign 26 · Sales 111 · Sales training 71 · Sandwich figure 16 · S-Bahn 75 · Scales 19 · Seal 19 · Secretary 113 · Self exploitation 87 · Self-Assessment 85 · Self-awareness 88 · Self-control 88 · Self-expression 85 · Self-image 86 · Self-love 82 · Self-motivation 87 · Self-reflection 86 · Seminar 71 · Senses 21 · Server 105 · Service point 74 · Service quality 119 · Shade 22 · Shareholder 110 · Shark 22 · Shipping 113 · Shower 25 · Shuttle 75 · Sign 15 · Sign 26 · Signpost 17 · Skull, head 26 · Small group work 68 · Socket 23 · Software 106 · Software development 106 · Solution 96 · Sound 74 · Speaking one language 92 · Specialist 87 · Speech bubble 16 · Speed 89 · Springboard 26 · Stamina 88 · Statement 62 · Stock market 123 · Stock market boom 123 · Stock market crash 123 · Storm cloud 16 · Storytelling 40, 66 · Strategy 111, 116 · Structures 120 · Submarine 22 · Subsidies 124 · Success 97 · Suggestion system 122 · Suitability test 69 · Summary 78 · Supervisory board 110 · Suppliers 114 · Supply Chain Management 113 · Surface 121 · Sustainability 124 · Sword 26 · SWOT 43 · Symbols · System 58 · Systematic structural listing 70 ›››**T**››› Tablecloth 57 · Talk 77 · Talk in plain English 92 · Talk to one another 92 · Target 102 · Taxi 75 · Tea 23, 76 · Team 94, 97 · Team coaching 98 · Team development 68 · Team play 90 · Team success 98 · Team-building 68 · Teamwork 68 · Technology 74 · Telephone 23 · Telephone centre 113 · Telephone training 71 · Text border · Thermometer 19 · Things in common 58 · Think global, act local 122 · Thinking outside the box 85 · Thoughts 93 · Time 60 · Time intervals 60 · Time management 101 · Time manager 101 · Timing 102 · Toilets 74 · Tolerance 94 · Tools 121 · Train 75 · Training 71 · Transfers 75 · Transport 112 · Tree 20 · Tree 39 · Trip through the imagination (imaginary journey) 67 · Troubleshooting 107 · T-shirt 23 ›››**U**››› Umbrella 22 · Upturn 123 · Use simple language 92 · User 107 ›››**V**››› Values 96 · View 49 · Visions 95, 96 · Visual Facilitation 67 · Visualize 60 ›››**W**››› Walk the talk 92 · Wall 97 · Wall calendar 23 · Warehouse 113 · Watering can 22 · Wavy arrow 17 · Way of thinking 48 · WC 74 · Weight 98 · Welcome poster 35 · Who is doing what by when 36 · Wilderness training 70 · Willingness to learn 85 · Willingness to take risks 88 · Win-Win situation 117 · Wireless network 105 · Work-life balance 84 · Works 110 · Works council 111 · Workshop 71 · World Café 42, 56, 66 · World Wide Web 106 · Wrapping up 78 · Writing workshop

››› Insider-Tipps
Insider-Tips

1 Machen Sie es sich leicht! Nutzen Sie Visualisierungen, die Ihnen leicht von der Hand gehen – vor allem wenn Sie mit einer Gruppe arbeiten. So geraten Sie nicht in Stress, und Sie werden visuell verstanden. Unser Tipp: Zuhause üben und bei der Arbeit möglichst innerhalb Ihres schnell abrufbaren Repertoirs bleiben!

1 Make it easy on yourself! Use visualizations which are easy for you, especially when working with a group. Otherwise you will get stressed. And your pictures will be understood. A tip from us: practise at home and, if possible, keep your work within the repertoire you can easily manage!

2 Finden Sie den kleinen Unterschied! Wenn Sie eine neue Figur, ein neues Symbol oder einen Text-Container üben und in Ihr Repertoire aufnehmen möchten, ist es hilfreich, wenn Sie sich die neue Form im Detail anschauen. Achten Sie auf Proportionen und einzelne Striche und Linien.
Üben Sie so lange, bis Sie den »Trick« bzw. den perfekten Strich herausfinden und erzielen Sie mit einem kleinen Unterschied eine große Wirkung.

2 Find the little difference! If you are practising a new symbol or a text border that you wish to include in your repertoire, it is helpful to look at the new shape in detail. Note the proportions and the individual pen strokes and lines. Practise until you have the 'trick' or the perfect way of drawing it, and you will achieve greater impact with a little practice.

3 Merken Sie sich Ihre Strichfolge! Jede Form, ob Symbol, Figur, Text-Container oder eine simple Grafik, zeichnen Sie am besten immer in der gleichen Strichfolge. Auf diese Weise gewinnen Sie an Schnelligkeit bei der Ausführung. Darüber hinaus werden Sie die meisten Formen über den ersten Strich sehr gut erinnern. Aus einer gezeichneten Spirale entsteht beispielsweise eine Papierrolle. Merken Sie sich diese ersten Strichfolgen, werden Sie immer schneller beim Live-Visualisieren und entwickeln Sie mit den ersten Strichen Ihre eigene Gedächtnishilfen.

3 Note the order of your pen strokes! The best way to draw any shape, whether it is a symbol, a figure, a text border or a simple graphic, is to always use the same pen strokes. This will help you pick up speed in your drawings. It will also mean that you remember most shapes as soon as you make the first stroke. For example, a spiral can turn into a role of paper. If you remember the first strokes, you will get quicker and quicker at live visualizing and you can develop your own memory aids with the first strokes.

Insider-Tipps
Insider-Tips

4 Nutzen Sie Farben. Aber mit System! Farben verschaffen Übersicht und Ordnung, indem sie z. B. einzelne Bereiche hervorheben und dadurch von anderen Bereichen trennen. Überschriften oder Unterpunkte können z.B. in einer Farbe erscheinen. So entwickelt sich ein roter Faden, dem das Auge gut folgen kann. Der Aufbau und die Logik Ihrer Visualisierung (z.B. ein Plakat) wird deutlich. Farben, die im Farbkreis direkt nebeneinander liegen (z.B. Orange/Gelb oder Violett/Rot) passen gut zueinander und lassen eine Visualisierung professioneller und ruhiger erscheinen als ein buntes Farbengewitter ohne Zusammenhang. Faustregel (damit es nicht zu bunt wird): Schwarz plus zwei Farben. Grau für Schatten geht immer.

4 Use colors. But consistently! Colors create order and make things clearer. They can be used for example, to highlight individual areas and separate them from other areas. For example, headings or subsidiary points can appear in one color. This provides a central line which it is easy for the eye to follow. The structure and logic of your visualization (e.g. a poster) becomes clear. Colors which are right next to one another in the color circle (e.g. orange/yellow or purple/red) work well together and make a visualization look more professional and calmer than a bright mish-mash of colors which do not tie together. Rule of thumb (so it does not get too colorful): black plus two colors. Grey can always be used for shadows.

5 Nutzen Sie Grau für Schatten und Lichteffekte! Jeder Visualisierung, und sei sie noch so einfach, verhelfen Sie durch ein paar Striche mit der Farbe Grau zu großer Wirkung. Dazu entscheiden Sie sich vorab, aus welche Richtung das Licht kommt bzw. die Sonne scheint (z.B. links oben), und dann wissen Sie mit ein wenig Übung auch schnell, wo ein Schatten entsteht. Grau ist die kleine Wunderwaffe für Visualisierer!

5 Use grey for shadows and light effect! The impact of any visualization, however simple, is improved by a couple of strokes in grey. To do this, you need to decide in advance what direction the light is coming in or the sun is shining (e.g. top left) and then, with just a little practice, you will know where the shadow will appear. Grey is a little miracle-worker for visualizers!

6 Schreiben Sie erst das Wort! Jede Form der Dekoration bzw. Hervorhebung kommt erst im zweiten Schritt dazu. Dies gilt für Farben (z.B. 3D-Schrift), Linien (z.B. Unterstreichungen) und vor allem für die so genannten Textcontainer. Als Textcontainer dient jede Form, die einen Text enthalten kann, wie z.B. eine Banderole, ein aufgeschlagenes Buch, ein Pfeil oder ein Schild. Schreiben Sie erst das Wort (z.B. eine Überschrift) und zeichnen Sie dann den Container herum. Auf diese Weise ist der Container immer passgenau.

6 Write the word first! Any form of decoration or emphasis should be the second stage. This applies to colors (e.g. 3D writing), lines (e.g. underlining) and, most importantly, for what are known as text borders. Text borders are any shape which can contain a text, such as a banner, an open book, an arrow or a sign. Write the word first (e.g. a header) and then draw the container around it. This ensures the border is always exactly the right size.

Insider-Tipps
Insider-Tips

7 Optimieren Sie Ihre Schrift! Eine professionelle Visualisierung kommt ganz besonders in der Schrift zum Ausdruck, denn es geht nicht um Bilderrätsel, sondern immer um sinnstiftende Wort-Bild-Kombinationen. Nehmen Sie sich daher ein wenig Zeit, um Ihre Schrift zu optimieren. Erlernen Sie die Moderationsschrift (Hand ruht auf dem Papier, kurze Über- bzw. Unterlängen, Buchstaben eng – aber nicht überlappend – aneinander, ausreichend Platz zwischen einzelnen Worten) oder optimieren Sie Ihren eigenen Stil. Unser Tipp: Sich nicht von der Gruppe im Rücken beunruhigen lassen. Nehmen Sie sich die Zeit – es lohnt sich!

8 Fertigen Sie vorher eine Skizze an! Große Formate und komplexere Layouts fordern unsere räumliche Vorstellungskraft heraus. Denn es braucht Übung, einzelne Formen, Gegenstände und Schrift auf einer großen Fläche harmonisch und sinnvoll anzuordnen. Wenn Sie vorab eine Skizze anfertigen, können Sie alles vorzeichnen und so lange probieren, bis es für Sie passt. Danach übertragen Sie Ihre Skizze auf den größeren Maßstab (ggf. mit Hilfe eines Rasters).

9 Nutzen Sie den ganzen Raum! Ihre Visualisierung gewinnt durch eine ausgewogene und dem Inhalt entsprechende Gesamtgestaltung der Fläche. Dies gilt besonders für komplexere Plakat-Layouts. Neben der Fläche spielt aber auch die Tiefe eine wichtige Rolle. Nutzen Sie die dritte Dimension und arbeiten Sie bewusst mit Vorder- und Hintergrund. Dabei geht es vor allem darum, »überlappend« zu visualisieren (was vorne ist, wird immer zuerst gezeichnet!) Üben Sie diese Effekte und entwickeln Sie den rechten Blick dafür, wann Ihnen diese Dimension hilft (z.B. ganz vorne: eine Figuren-Gruppe, dahinter: ein Gebäude mit Schildern, dahinter ein Weg und ganz hinten der Horizont, usw.).

7 Work on your writing! Professional visualization is most clearly expressed in your writing – it should not be a jumble of pictures, more a sensible combination of words and pictures. So take a little time to work on your writing. Learn moderation writing (hand resting on the paper, short up and down-strokes, letters close together (but not overlapping!), sufficient space between individual words) or optimise your own style. A tip from us: do not let the group behind you put you off. Take your time – it's worth it!

8 Produce a sketch beforehand! Large formats and complex layouts challenge our sense of spatial imagination. After all, it takes practice to arrange individual shapes, objects and writing harmoniously and sensibly across a wide area. If you produce a sketch in advance, you can draw everything first and keep practising until it works for you. Then you can transfer your sketch to a larger scale (using a grid if necessary).

9 Use all of the space! Your visualization will benefit from a balanced overall use of the space in accordance with the content. This is especially true for more complex poster layouts. As well as the area, depth of field also plays an important role. Use the third dimension and work consciously with foreground and background. The main thing is to visualize on an «overlapping» base (the foreground is always drawn first!) Practise these effects and develop a good eye for when this dimension will help you (e.g. right in front, a group of figures, behind, a building with signs, then a path and right at the back, the horizon, etc.).

A

Die wichtigsten Zutaten für Visual Facilitating

The most important ingredients for Visual Facilitating

A1 Textcontainer
Text Borders

Einzelne, wichtige Begriffe, wie z.B. Überschriften, längere Texte, eine Feedback-Sammlung (O-Töne) oder Spielregeln, heben Sie durch so genannte Textcontainer hervor.

Ein Textcontainer kann jede beliebige Form haben: Ein rechteckiger Kasten (als Schild), in Form eines Pfeils oder einfach kreisrund. Oder Sie verwenden Gegenstände und Symbole als Textcontainer: z.B. ein aufgeschlagenes Buch, einen Notiz-Zettel oder eine Wolke! Sehr beliebt sind auch Banner, Banderolen und Papierrollen.

Nutzen Sie Textcontainer, um Inhalte in Form zu bringen und Aussagen hervorzuheben. Gestalten Sie ein Plakat, z.B. für Flipcharts und Pinwände, durch eine geschickte Anordnung unterschiedlicher Textcontainer und sorgen Sie somit für Übersicht.

Important, individual terms, such as headings, longer texts, a collection of feedback (quotables) or rules can be highlighted using what are known as text borders.

Text borders come in all shapes and sizes. Graphical: e.g. a square box (as a sign), an arrow or simply a circle. Or you can use objects and symbols as text containers: e.g. an open book, a sheet of notepaper or a cloud! Banners and rolls of paper are also very popular.

Use text border to bring life to content and emphasise statements. Design a poster, e.g. for flip charts and pin boards, by cleverly arranging different text borders to give a clear overview.

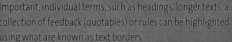

A1 Textcontainer
Text Borders

A1 Textcontainer
Text Borders

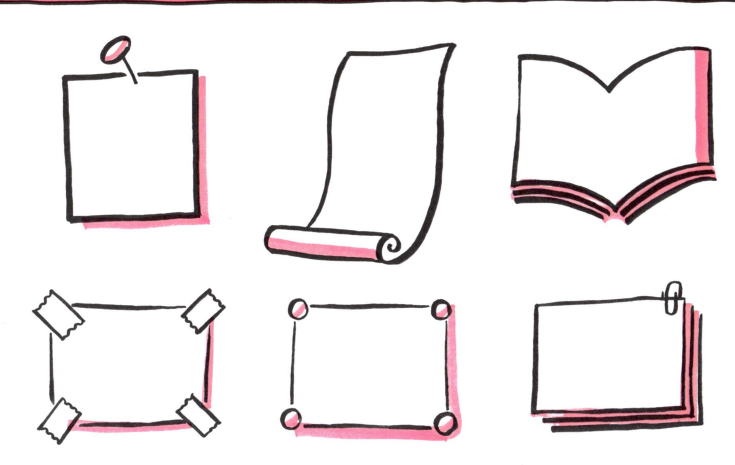

A1 Textcontainer
Text Borders

A1 Textcontainer
Text Borders

A1 Textcontainer
Text Borders

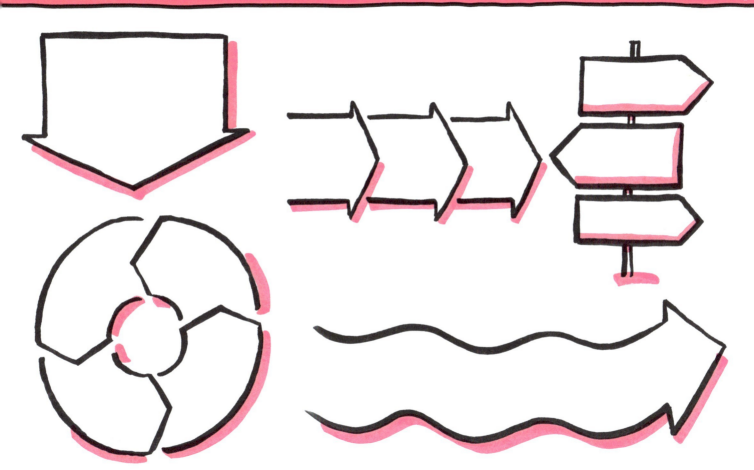

A2 Symbole
Symbols

Hier finden Sie eine Zusammenstellung der bewährtesten Symbole aus der Visualisierungspraxis der Kommunikationslotsen. Symbole sind oftmals Gegenstände, denen eine weitere Bedeutung zugeordnet wird: In der Welt der Visualisierung steht z.B. eine Glühbirne selten für eine Glühbirne oder elektrisches Licht, sondern für Idee/Ideenreichtum oder Kreativität. Symbole verwenden Sie, um Themen, Stimmungen und Aussagen zu verdeutlichen. In Kombination mit grafischen Elementen (z.B. einem Kreis) entstehen daraus u. a. sehr brauchbare Textcontainer mit einem zusätzlichen Informationsgehalt (z.B. ein Kreis mit einer Glühbirne = Textcontainer für Ideensammlung).

Die Kunst liegt in der richtigen Kombination und Anordnung. Kombinieren und rekombinieren Sie einfach mal drauf los und entdecken Sie immer wieder neue Bedeutungen. Was könnte man wohl aus einem Herz und einer Flamme machen? Aus einem Gebäude und einem Qualitätssiegel?

Der Phantasie sind hier keine Grenzen gesetzt. Oftmals gilt aber auch: Weniger ist mehr. Ein ansehnliches Flipchart-Plakat entsteht bereits, wenn Sie mit einem Strich in Schwarz oder Grau einen Rahmen ziehen und zentral oben oder unten rechts auf den Rahmen ein Symbol setzen. Fertig. Es kann so einfach sein!

This is a summary of the most established symbols from visualization out of Kommunikationslotsen practice. Symbols are often objects, for example, in the world of visualization, a light bulb rarely represents a light bulb or electric light, it is more a symbol of ideas/inventiveness or creativity. Use symbols to clarify subjects, moods and statements. In combination with graphical elements (e.g. a circle), this can produce a number of things, including very usable text borders with additional information content (e.g. a circle with a light bulb = text container for collection of ideas).

The art is in getting the combination and arrangement right. Just try combining and re-combining and discover all sorts of new meanings. What could you do with a heart and a flame? With a building and a quality seal? There are no limits to your imagination. However, it is often true to say that less is more. You can produce a decent flipchart poster by drawing a frame in black or grey and then putting a symbol in the centre at the top or in the bottom right. That's all! It can be that simple!

A2 Symbole
Symbols

A2 Symbole
Symbols

A2 Symbole
Symbols

A2 Symbole
Symbols

A2 Symbole / Symbols

A2 Symbole
Symbols

A2 Symbole
Symbols

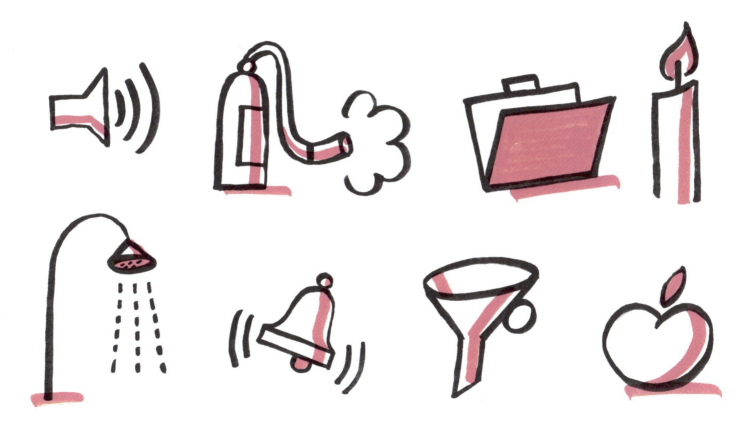

A2 Symbole / Symbols

A3 Figuren
Figures

Figuren spielen in der Welt der Visualisierung eine wichtige Rolle. Wenn Sie z. B. über verschiedene Arbeitsbereiche, Führungsebenen oder Zielgruppen sprechen, ist es sehr hilfreich, ein paar Figuren parat zu haben. Denn sie führen Handlungen aus und sind Platzhalter für Einzelpersonen, Teams und Gruppen.

Im ersten bikablo® finden Sie Standardfiguren, verschiedene Stile (z.B. Starpeople, MW-Figuren) und Typen (Männlein, Weiblein, Familien, verschiedene Berufe, etc.). In dem vorliegenden Kapitel gehen wir einen Schritt weiter und bringen die Figuren in Bewegung. Hier finden Sie auf das Wesentliche reduzierte Figuren (ohne Gesicht und Mimik). Wie immer bei visuellen Codes, geht es nicht um die realistische Darstellung, sondern um eine auf den ersten Blick erkennbare Situation bzw. Aussage. Dafür reichen in der Regel eine spezifische Körperhaltung und Gestik.

Besondere Effekte erzielen Sie, wenn Sie Figuren mit Symbolen und Gegenständen kombinieren. Mit ein paar »Speedlines« (Bewegungsstrichen) beeinflussen Sie die Art der jeweiligen Bewegung bzw. Aktion noch zusätzlich. Denn Sie verstärken dadurch Bewegungen (schnell, langsam, vibrierend, aufprallend) und Emotionen (Wut, Erstaunen, Überraschung).

Figures play an important role in the world of visualization. If, for example, you are talking about different departments, management levels or target groups, it is very useful to have a couple of figures ready. They carry out actions and act as placeholders for individuals, teams and groups.

The first bikablo® contains standard figures of various styles (e.g. star people, MW figures) and types (man, woman, family, different professions, etc.) In this chapter, we care going a step further and getting the figures to move. The figures here are reduced to a bare minimum (without face or expressions).
As always with visual codes, it is not about producing a realistic representation, instead it should be a situation or statement which is apparent from the first glance. This can normally be conveyed with a specific body posture or gesture.

It is particularly effective to combine figures with symbols and objects. A couple of 'speed lines' have an additional effect on the nature of the relevant movement of actions. They also emphasise movements (fast, slow, vibrating, impact) and emotions (angry, shocked, surprised).

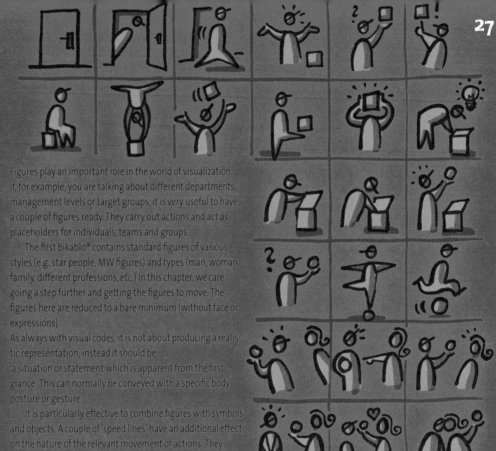

A3 Figuren / Figures

A3 Figuren / Figures

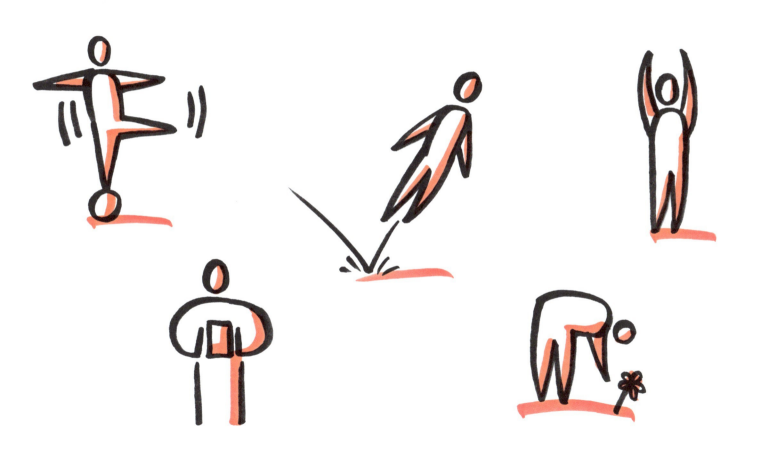

A3 Figuren / Figures

30

A3 Figuren / Figures

A3 Figuren / Figures

A3 Figuren / Figures

A4 Layouts für Flipchart und Pinwand
Layouts for flip charts and pin boards

Jede Visualisierung beruht auf einer Anordnung einzelner Elemente (Schrift, Grafik, Symbole, etc.). Ist die Anordnung stimmig, können Sie von einem guten Layout bzw. Plakat sprechen.

Nutzen Sie unsere Vorlagen, um Flipcharts und Pinwandplakate zu entwickeln, die Ihren jeweiligen Lern- oder Dialogprozess unterstützen. Sie finden einfache Präsentationsplakate, um beispielsweise Spielregeln oder eine Agenda ins rechte Bild zu rücken. Darüber hinaus haben sich Plakate bewährt, die nur zum Teil vorbereitet (Überschrift, Rahmen, ggf. ein Symbol) und dann gemeinsam mit der Gruppe fertiggestellt werden. Sammeln Sie beispielsweise O-Töne, Feedback und Meinungen, schreiben Sie diese in Ihr vorbereitetes Plakat, dann noch schnell ein paar Symbole, Figuren oder Container dazu (z.B. O-Töne in einer Sprechblase) – fertig!

Überlegen Sie auch, an welcher Stelle im Dialogprozess die Teilnehmer bei der Visualisierung beteiligt werden können. Kombinieren Sie verschiedene Vorlagen und stellen Sie Ihr eigenes Set an Plakaten zusammen (z.B. für Meeting, Konferenz, Training, Changeprozess).

Sollten Sie einzelne Methoden oder Prozessschritte, die wir im Folgenden erwähnen, nicht kennen, so macht das gar nichts – nutzen Sie die Layouts einfach als Inspirationsquelle für Ihre eigene Vorgehensweise und Ihr persönliches Methodenrepertoir!

All visualization is based on arranging individual elements (writing, graphics, symbols, etc.). If the arrangement makes sense, it is considered a good layout or poster.

Use our templates to develop flip charts and pin board poster to support your own learning or dialogue processes. You can find simple presentation posters to emphasise, for example, rules or an agenda. Posters which are only partially prepared (headline, frame, symbol if necessary) and then completed with the group have also proven successful. For example, collect quotables, feedback and opinions, write these into your prepared poster, then just quickly add a couple of symbols, figures or borders (e.g. quotables in a speech bubble) – and you're done!

Also think about which points in the dialogue process the participants can be involved in visualization. Combine various templates and put together your own set of posters (e.g. for a meeting, conference, training course or change process).

If you are not familiar with individual methods or process stages mentioned below, it doesn't matter – simply use the layouts as a source of inspiration for your own approach and your personal repertoire of methods!

A4 Layouts
Layouts
› Standardplakate für jede Gelegenheit
› Standard posters for all occasions

Willkommensplakat

Welcome poster

Agenda

Agenda

Vereinbarung von Spielregeln

Agreement of rules

A4 Layouts
Layouts

› Standardplakate für jede Gelegenheit
› Standard posters for all occasions

36

Vorstellung oder Sammlung von Themen und Inhalten

Vorstellung oder Sammlung von Lernschritten

Vereinbarung: Wer macht was bis wann?

Presentation or collection of themes and contents

Presentation or collection of learning stages

Agreement: Who is doing what by when?

A4 Layouts
Layouts › Plakate für Beiträge aus der Gruppe

Ideensammlung

Collection of ideas

Sammlung von Feedback oder Learnings

Collection of feedback or what has been learnt

Mindmapping

Mind mapping

A4 Layouts

› Plakate für Prozessplanung (Roadmaps)

38

Roadmap als Straße zum Horizont:
Ist-Zustand · Ressourcen · Meilensteine · Hindernisse · Herausforderungen · To-Do-Liste · Ziel
Roadmap as a street to a horizon:
Current status · Resources · Milestones · Obstacles · Challenges · To-do list · Objective

Roadmap als Bergwanderung:
Ist-Zustand · Zwischenschritte · Ziel
Roadmap as a mountain hike:
Current situation · Interim steps · Target

Roadmap als Weg durch Landschaft:
Startpunkt · Zwischenschritte · Ziel
Roadmap as path trough landscape:
Starting point · Interim steps · Target

A4 Layouts › Plakate zur Themenerkundung

Erkundung eines Unternehmens oder Projektes als Baum:
Ressourcen (Wurzeln) · Entwicklungsschritte (Stamm) ·
Investitionen (Gießkanne) · Erträge (Äpfel)

Investigating a company or project as a tree:
Resources · (roots) · Development steps (trunk) ·
Investments (watering can) · Revenue (apples)

Erkundung eines Lernfeldes:
Wie tief wollen wir ins Thema einsteigen?

Exploring a learning environment:
How deep do we want to get into the subject?

Erkundung eines Themas oder Zustands:
Was erkennen wir an der Oberfläche?
Was vermuten wir unter der Oberfläche?

Exploring a subject or situation:
What can we recognise from the surface?
What can we guess is below the surface?

A4 Layouts
› Plakate für Kleingruppenarbeit
› Posters for small group work

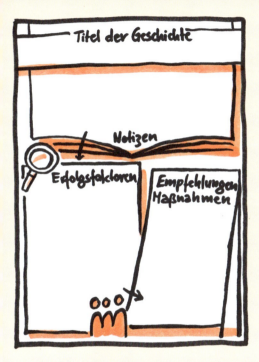

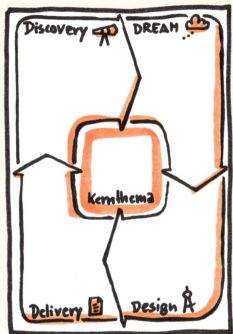

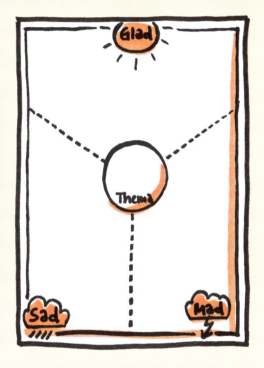

Appreciative Inquiry (AI)- bzw. Storytelling: Titel (der Geschichte) · Was geschah? (Notizen) · Was hat es ermöglicht? (Erfolgsfaktoren) · Empfehlungen/Maßnahmen für die Zukunft
Appreciative Inquiry (AI) or storytelling: Title (of the story) · What happened? (Notes) · What made it possible? (Success factors) · Recommendations/Measures for the future

Appreciative Inquiry-4D-Zyklus:
Kernthema (Mitte) · Discovery · Dream · Design · Delivery
Appreciative Inquiry-4D-Cycle:
Topic (Middle) · Discovery · Dream · Design · Delivery

Gruppenarbeit: Thema/These ·
Was stimmt uns froh? · Was stimmt uns eher traurig? ·
Was macht uns wütend/rasend?
Group work:
Subject/Hypothesis · What makes us glad? ·
What makes us sad? · What makes us angry/mad?

A4 Layouts
› Plakate für Kleingruppenarbeit
› Posters for small group work

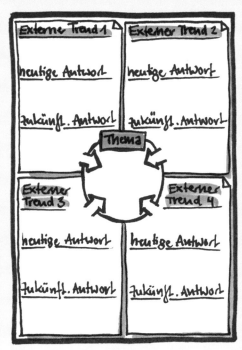

Offenes Forum:
Was haben wir gehört? · Welche Reaktion haben wir darauf? ·
Welche Verständnisfragen haben wir? An wen?
Open forum: What have we heard? ·
What is our reaction to it? · What questions do we have on
understanding? · To whom?

Zukunftskonferenz:
Externe Trends · Heutige & künftige Antworten

Future Search:
External trends · Current and future answers

Zukunftskonferenz:
Team · Teilnehmer · Stolz & Bedauern

Future Search:
Team · Participants · Proud & Sorry

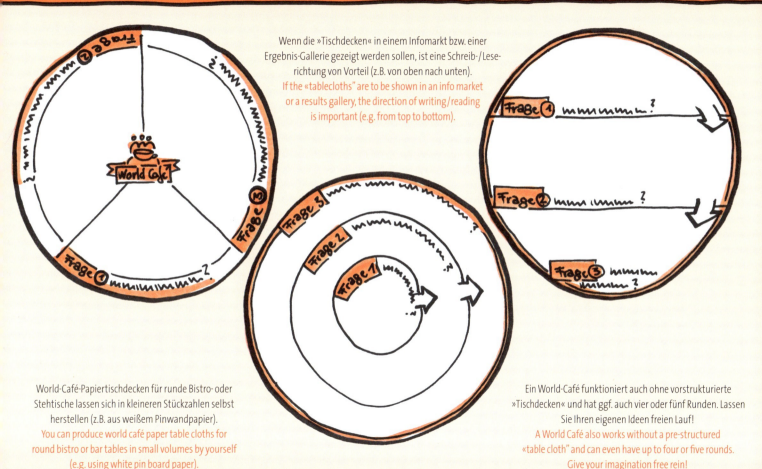

A4 Layouts
Layouts
› Ergebnisplakate für Workshops
› Workshop results posters

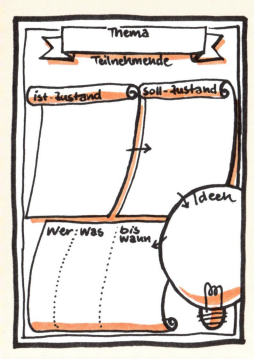

Unser Klassiker: Für Open Space-Workshops oder andere Verfahren. Gibt es auch bei Neuland vorproduziert als Flipchart-Block (Art. 8103.701).

Our classics: For open space workshops or other processes. Can also be bought from Neuland as a pre-made flip-chart block (Item 8103.701).

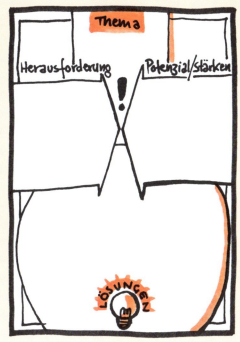

Workshopergebnisplakat: Thema · Herausforderungen · Potential/Stärken · Lösungen

Workshop results poster:
Subject · Challenges · Potential/Strengths · Solutions

SWOT-Analyse:
Stärken · Schwächen · Chancen · Risiken

SWOT-Analysis:
Strenghts · Weaknesses · Opportunities · Threats

A4 Layouts
Layouts
› Projektplanungsplakate
› Project planning posters

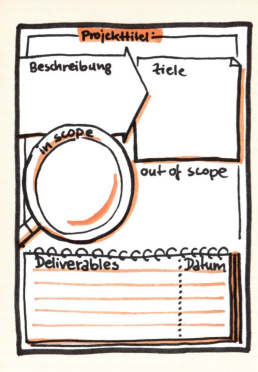
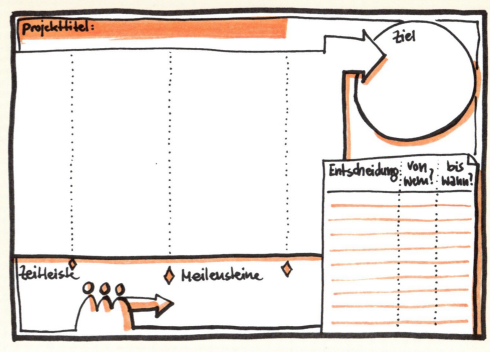

Projekttitel · Projektbeschreibung & Hintergrund · Ziele · In Scope/Out of Scope · zu liefernde Ergebnisse (Deliverables) und Datum

Project title · Project description & background · Objectives In Scope/Out of Scope · results to be achieved · (Deliverables) and date

Projekttitel · Zeitleiste & Meilensteine für Maßnahmen · Ziel, erforderliche Entscheidung(en) von wem bis wann

Project title · Timeline and milestones for measures · Aim, decision(s) necessary by whom by when

A4 Layouts
› Projektplanungsplakate
› Project planning posters

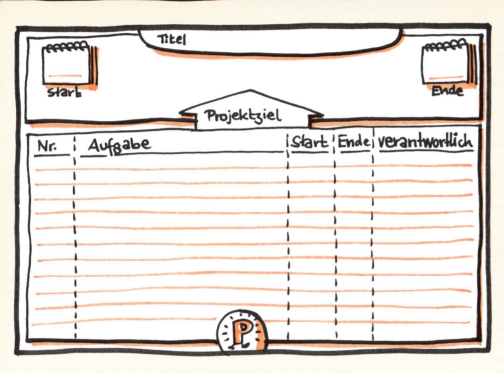

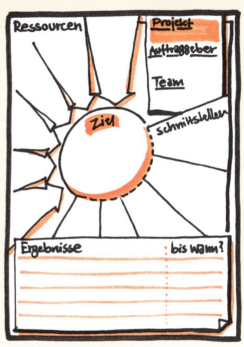

Projekttitel · Projektziel(e) · Start · Ende · Aufgaben 1-10 ·
Start-Datum · Ende-Datum · Tage/Aufwand · Verantwortlichkeit

Project title · Project aim(s) · Start · End · Tasks 1-10 ·
Start date · End date · Days/Expense · Responsibility

Projekttitel · Auftraggeber · Projektteam ·
Projektanlass & -Ziel · Ressourcen · Schnittstellen ·
Ergebnisse und bis wann
Project title · Customer · Project Team ·
Project occasion & objective · Resources · Interfaces ·
Results and by when

B

Workshop, Meeting, Seminar und Training

Workshops, meetings, seminars and training courses

B1 Prinzipien und Spielregeln
Principles and rules

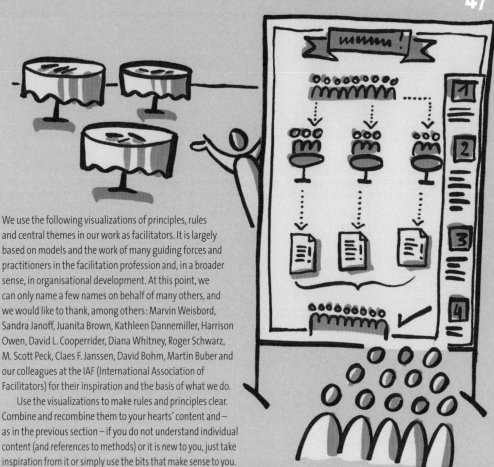

Die folgenden Visualisierungen von Prinzipien, Spielregeln und Leitgedanken verwenden wir in unserer Arbeit als Facilitator. Sie beruhen überwiegend auf Modellen und der Arbeit vieler Vordenker, Praktiker und Praktikerinnen der Profession Facilitation und im weitesten Sinne Organizational Development. Wir können an dieser Stelle nur einige stellvertretend für viele andere nennen und danken u. a. Marvin Weisbord, Sandra Janoff, Juanita Brown, Kathleen Dannemiller, Harrison Owen, David L. Cooperrider, Diana Whitney, Roger Schwarz, M. Scott Peck, Claes F. Janssen, David Bohm, Martin Buber und unseren Kollegen der IAF (International Association of Facilitators) für die Inspiration und Grundlagen unseres Wirkens.

Nutzen Sie die Visualisierungen, um Spielregeln und Prinzipien zu verdeutlichen. Kombinieren und rekombinieren Sie nach Herzenslust. Wie im vorherigen Abschnitt gilt: sollten einzelne Inhalte (und Hinweise auf Methoden) für Sie neu oder unverständlich sein, lassen Sie sich inspirieren oder nutzen Sie einfach das, was für Sie Sinn macht.

We use the following visualizations of principles, rules and central themes in our work as facilitators. It is largely based on models and the work of many guiding forces and practitioners in the facilitation profession and, in a broader sense, in organisational development. At this point, we can only name a few names on behalf of many others, and we would like to thank, among others: Marvin Weisbord, Sandra Janoff, Juanita Brown, Kathleen Dannemiller, Harrison Owen, David L. Cooperrider, Diana Whitney, Roger Schwarz, M. Scott Peck, Claes F. Janssen, David Bohm, Martin Buber and our colleagues at the IAF (International Association of Facilitators) for their inspiration and the basis of what we do.

Use the visualizations to make rules and principles clear. Combine and recombine them to your hearts' content and – as in the previous section – if you do not understand individual content (and references to methods) or it is new to you, just take inspiration from it or simply use the bits that make sense to you.

B1 Prinzipien und Spielregeln › Dialog
Principles and rules › Dialogue

Ich verstehe mich als Lernender und Erkundender (im Gegensatz zum Wissenden).
I consider myself a learner and an explorer (by contrast to a knower).

Ich achte dich und versuche, die Welt aus deiner Perspektive zu sehen.
I respect you and am trying to see the world from your perspective.

Ich teile mich offen mit und bin offen, mich von deiner Denkweise beeinflussen zu lassen.
I am communicating openly and am open to being influenced by your way of thinking.

Annahmen offen legen und in der Schwebe halten.
Present assumptions and hold them in the balance

B1 Prinzipien und Spielregeln › Dialog
Principles and rules › Dialogue

Ich weiß um die verändernde Kraft des Zuhörens!
I know about the changing power of listening!

Ich gehe nicht von der Annahme aus, dass schneller besser ist.
I do not assume that faster is better.

Ich weiß, dass meine Sichtweise nicht die einzig mögliche ist.
I know that my view is not the only one possible.

Manchmal ist es wichtiger zu beobachten, wie wir aufeinander reagieren.
Sometimes, it is more important to observe how we react to one another.

B1 Prinzipien und Spielregeln / Principles and rules
› Facilitation, Prozessberatung, Moderation
› Facilitation, process consultancy, moderation

Facilitator: Experte für den Prozess/die Methode. Teilnehmer: Experten für den Inhalt.
Facilitator: Process/method expert. Participants: Content experts.

Vertraue dem Prozess.
Trust the process.

Das Wissen liegt im System.
The knowledge is in the system.

Jede Frage beinhaltet bereits die Antwort.
Every question already includes the answer.

B1 Prinzipien und Spielregeln / Principles and rules
› Facilitation, Prozessberatung, Moderation
› Facilitation, process consultancy, moderation

Eine gute Frage ist oftmals wichtiger als eine gute Antwort.
A good question is often more important than a good answer.

Jede Frage ist eine Intervention.
Every question is an intervention.

Man kann nicht nicht kommunizieren.
You cannot not communicate.

Den ganzen Elefanten erkunden.
Exploring the whole elephant.

Vierraum-Wohnung: Change-Theorie (Zufriedenheit · Leugnung · Konfusion · Erneuerung)
Four Rooms of Change theory (Contentment · Denial · Confusion · Renewal)

B1 Prinzipien und Spielregeln › Open Space
Principles and rules › Open Space Technology

Wer auch immer kommt, es ist der/die Richtige!
Whoever comes is the right one!

Was auch immer geschieht, es ist das einzige, was geschehen kann!
Whatever happens, it is the only thing that can happen!

Wann immer es beginnt, es ist die richtige Zeit!
Whenever it begins is the right time!

Wenn es vorbei ist, ist es vorbei! (Und: Nicht vorbei, ist nicht vorbei!)
When it is over, it is over! (and: not over is not over!)

B1 Prinzipien und Spielregeln › Open Space
Principles and rules › Open Space Technology

Gesetz der zwei Füße
Law of two feet

Zwei Erscheinungen: Hummeln und Schmetterlinge
Two phenomena: Bumble bees and butterflies

Eine Ermahnung: Seien Sie bereit, überrascht zu werden!
One admonition: be prepared to be surprised!

Die wichtigsten Gespräche finden in der Kaffeepause statt.
The most important conversations take place during coffee breaks.

B1 Prinzipien und Spielregeln › Appreciative Inquiry
Principles and rules › Appreciative Inquiry

Das, worauf wir unsere Beobachtungen richten, wird unsere Realität.
What our observations are focussed on becomes our reality.

Realität entsteht im Moment, und es gibt viele (multiple) Realitäten.
Reality happens in the moment, and there are multiple realities.

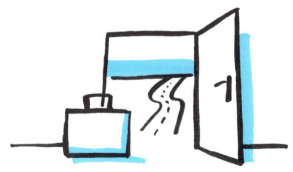

Wer in die Zukunft geht, hat mehr Vertrauen, wenn er Teile der Vergangenheit mitnimmt ...
Anyone going into the future has more confidence if he takes part of the past with him ...

... und sollte das mitnehmen, was das Beste der Vergangenheit war.
... and we should take with us the best of the past.

B1 Prinzipien und Spielregeln › Appreciative Inquiry
Principles and rules › Appreciative Inquiry

In jeder Gesellschaft, Organisation oder Gruppe gibt es etwas, was funktioniert.
In every society, organisation or group, there is something that works.

Dass wir eine Frage stellen, hat bereits eine Auswirkung (es gibt keine neutralen Fragen).
The fact that we ask a question already has consequences (there are no neutral questions).

Es ist wichtig, Unterschiede zu würdigen.
It is important to respect differences.

Die Sprache, die wir benutzen, kreiert unsere Realität.
The language we use creates our reality.

B1 Prinzipien und Spielregeln › World Café
Principles and rules › World Café

Lenken Sie Ihren Fokus auf das, was wichtig ist.
Focus on the things that are important.

Tragen sie eigene Sichtweisen bei.
Add your own perspectives.

Sprechen und hören Sie mit Herz und Verstand.
Talk and listen with your heart and your mind.

Hören Sie genau hin, um wirklich zu verstehen.
Listen properly so you really understand.

B1 Prinzipien und Spielregeln › World Café
Principles and rules › World Café

Verbinden sie Ideen miteinander.
Connect ideas with one another.

Richten Sie Ihre Aufmerksamkeit auf neue Erkenntnisse und tiefergehende Fragen.

Spielen, kritzeln und malen Sie – auf die Tischdecke schreiben ist erwünscht!
Play, scribble and paint – writing on the tablecloth is the idea!

Haben Sie Spaß dabei!
And have fun doing it!

B1 Prinzipien und Spielregeln / Principles and rules
› Zukunftskonferenz
› Future Search

das ganze, offene System in einen Raum holen
Bringing the "Whole system" in the room

Gemeinsamkeiten finden statt Konflikte bearbeiten
Finding things in common instead of working through conflicts

erst Konsens erreichen, dann Maßnahmen planen
Reaching a consensus first, then planning measures

in selbststeuernden Gruppen arbeiten
Working in independent groups

B1 Prinzipien und Spielregeln › Zukunftskonferenz
Principles and rules › Future Workshop

alle Meinungen sind gültig
All opinions are valid.

Differenzen würdigen und erkunden, aber nicht bearbeiten
Respect and explore differences, but do not tackle them.

den Fokus auf die Zukunft statt auf die Probleme richten
Put the focus on the future instead of the problems

B1 Prinzipien und Spielregeln / Principles and rules
› Zukunftswerkstatt Einführung / Future Workshop introduction

Arbeitsteilung Facilitator/Moderator und Gruppe
Work share between facilitator/moderator and group.

kurze Zeitintervalle
Short time intervals

Pausen
Breaks

kreative Aktionen gehören dazu
Creative action is part of it

alle Inhalte/Ergebnisse visualisieren
Visualize all content/events

› Zukunftswerkstatt Kritikphase
› Future workshop criticism phase

nur Negatives zählt
Only negative things count

alles aufschreiben
Write everything down

sich kurz fassen
Keep it short

beim Thema bleiben
Stick to the subject

Erfahrungen und konkrete Beispiele berichten
Report experiences and concrete examples

B1 Prinzipien und Spielregeln / Principles and rules
› Zukunftswerkstatt Phantasiephase
› Future workshop imagination phase

nur Positives zählt
Only positive things count

alles ist möglich
Everything is possible

auf die Aussagen der anderen aufbauen
Build on others' statements

keine Killerphrasen
No killer phrases

| B1 **Prinzipien und Spielregeln** › Zukunftswerkstatt Realisierungsphase
Principles and rules › Future workshop implementation phase

Maßnahmen planen
Plan measures

Spezifisch sein · sich klar ausdrücken
Be specific · express yourself clearly

Realität einbeziehen
Include reality

an Zielen arbeiten
Work on objectives

B1 Prinzipien und Spielregeln › Community Building
Principles and rules › Community building

erst Gemeinschaft bilden, dann Entscheidungen treffen
Community Building first. Decision Making second.

Sprich nur, wenn Du bewegt bist, zu sprechen.
Only speak when you feel moved to speak.

Verwende Ich-Aussagen.
Use I statements.

Stelle deinen Namen voran, bevor Du sprichst.
Say your name first before you speak.

B2 Methoden und Techniken
Methods and techniques

Im letzten Abschnitt ging es um Prinzipien, Spielregeln und Grundhaltungen. Im folgenden Kapitel haben wir Logos und Piktogramme für viele bekannte Methoden und Techniken entworfen. Gestalten Sie damit ein Willkommensplakat, erläutern Sie anhand einer live erstellten Visualisierung den nächsten methodischen Schritt oder verschaffen Sie einer Gruppe über Bilder einen Überblick des gesamten Dialog- und Lernprozesses.

Gestalten Sie individuelle Tagungsunterlagen/Handouts, entwickeln Sie eigene Aktions- oder Programm-Logos und versehen Sie Ihr nächstes Projekt mit einem unverwechselbaren Design. Wiedererkennung durch Visualisierungen und piktogramm-ähnliche Zeichen sind gerade in Organisationen, in denen viel parallel läuft, gut für die eigene Orientierung und das interne Marketing. Und dabei ist Selbstgemachtes absolut empfehlenswert, denn es geht in der Regel um eine temporäre, teilweise sehr kurzfristige Konzentration auf ein Thema/ein Projekt und dafür können Sie ab jetzt den Aufwand in Grenzen halten. Do it yourself!

In the last section, we dealt with principles, rules and basic attitudes. In this chapter, we have put together logos and pictograms for many known methods and techniques. Use these to design a welcome poster, explain the next stage of the method by visualizing live or use pictures to give an overview of the entire dialogue and learning process for a group. Design individual conference documents/handouts, develop your own campaign or programme logos and give your next project an unmistakeable design. Especially in organisations where there are lots of things going on at once, recognition through visualization and pictogram-like symbols is good for your own orientation and for internal marketing. And something home made is definitely recommended, often it is just a temporary, sometimes very short term focus on a subject/project and this will help to keep costs within limits.. Do it yourself!

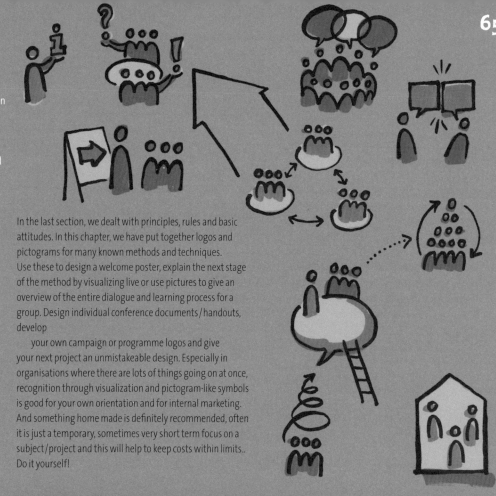

| **B2** | **Methoden und Techniken** | › Dialogmethoden/Grossgruppenverfahren |
| | **Methods and techniques** | › Dialogue methods/large group process |

Open Space
Open Space

World Café
World Café

Appreciative Inquiry
Appreciative Inquiry

Zukunftskonferenz
Future Search

Zukunftswerkstatt
Future Workshop

Storytelling
Storytelling

| B2 Methoden und Techniken | › Dialog- und Kreativitätstechniken |
| Methods and techniques | › Dialogue and creativity techniques |

Visualisierung
Visual Facilitation

Brainstorming
Brainstorming

Mindmapping
Mind mapping

Phantasiereise
Trip through the imagination

Infomarkt · Vernissage · Galerie
Information market · Private view · Gallery

Fish Bowl
Fish Bowl

B2 Methoden und Techniken › Workshop- und Trainingstechniken
Methods and techniques › Workshop and training techniques

Einstieg ins Thema
Entry into subject

2er/3er Interview
2/3 interviews

Gruppen- bzw. Kleingruppenarbeit · Teamarbeit
Group or small group work · teamwork

Teambuilding · Teamentwicklung
Team-building · Team development

Ergebnispräsentation
Presentation of results

Blitzpräsentation
Lightning presentation

B2 Methoden und Techniken › Workshop- und Trainingstechniken
Methods and techniques › Workshop and training techniques

Energizer
Energizer

Feedback · Rückmeldung
Feedback · evaluation

360 Grad-Feedback
360 degree Feedback

Assessment · Eignungstest
Assessment · Suitability test

Auswertung · Evaluation · Review
Evaluation · Review

B2 Methoden und Techniken › Workshop- und Trainingstechniken
Methods and techniques › Workshop and training techniques

Kreativ-Werkstatt · Schreibwerkstatt
Creative workshop · Writing workshop

Outdoor · Naturerfahrung · Wildnistraining
Outdoor · Nature experience · wilderness training

Aufstellung · Familienaufstellung · Systemische Strukturaufstellung
Listing · Family listing · Systematic structural listing

Organisationsaufstellung
Organisation list

B2 Methoden und Techniken › Trainingsinhalte
Methods and techniques › Training content

Seminar · Workshop · Training
Seminar · Workshop · Training

Verhaltenstraining
Behaviour training

Kommunikationstraining
Communication training

Verkaufstraining
Sales training

Telefontraining
Telephone training

EDV-Training
IT training

Produkt-Training
Product training

B3 Seminare und Konferenzen
Seminars and conferences

Hier finden Sie Bildvorlagen der häufigsten Themen und Begriffe rund um die Organisation, den Ablauf und das Rahmenprogramm von Seminaren und Konferenzen.

Nutzen Sie einzelne Visualisierungen zur Auszeichnung von Seminarräumen oder als Leitsystem in Tagungsstätten (z.B. Wegweiser). Verwenden Sie diese und ähnliche Visualisierungen auf Postern oder (Papier-)Bannern, um größere Gruppen durch die Agenda einer Konferenz zu leiten (Beispiel: »Infomarkt: Hier geht's lang!«). Denn wenn Sie Ihre TeilnehmerInnen mit einem visuellen Leitsystem und einem guten Gesamt-Design durch eine Tagung oder Konferenz begleiten, sichern Sie sich nicht nur einen besseren Verlauf Ihrer Veranstaltung, sondern fördern auch bessere Ergebnisse.

Wertvolle Unterstützung bieten die einzelnen Bilder auch bei der Seminar- und Konferenzplanung. Zeichnen Sie alle wesentlichen Themen und Begriffe auf Karten, nutzen Sie diese für das nächste Planungsgespräch in Ihrer Projektgruppe und erleben Sie, wie viel Spaß es machen kann, eine Veranstaltung bzw. ein Programm visuell zu konzipieren.

Here, you can find picture templates for the most frequent themes and terms you come across in organisations, in executing plans and and conferences.

Use individual visualizations to display in seminar rooms or as a guide system in conference locations (e.g. signposts). Use these and similar visualizations on posters or (paper) banners to guide large groups through a conference agenda (example: «Information market: this way!"). After all, if you can use a visual guide system and a good overall design to lead your delegates through a conference or congress, you can ensure not only that your event runs more smoothly, you can also promote better results.

The individual pictures also provide valuable support when it comes to seminar and conference planning. Draw all the important subjects and terms on cards, use these for the next planning meeting in your project group and experience how much fun it can be to visualize an event or a programme.

B3 Seminare und Konferenzen › Organisation
Seminars and conferences › Organisation

Meeting · Besprechung
Meeting

Moderator · Moderation
Moderator · Facilitator

Protokoll · Dokumentation
Protocol · Documentation

Tagungsunterlagen · Handout
Conference paperwork · Handout

Orgateam
Organisational team

Steuerungsgruppe
Control group

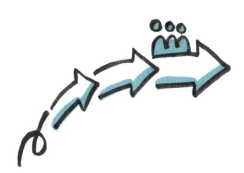

Pilotgruppe
Pilot group

B3 Seminare und Konferenzen / Seminars and conferences
› Organisation / Organisation

Technik: Sound · Mikrofon · Licht · Projektion
Technology: Sound Microphone · Lighting · Projecting

Toiletten · WC
Toilets · WC

Hostessen · Informationsschalter · Service-Point
Hostesses · Information desk · Service point

Check-in · Registrierung
Check-in · Registration

Namensschild
Name badge

B3 Seminare und Konferenzen › Organisation
Seminars and conferences › Organisation

Parkplatz
Car park

Transfer · Shuttle
Transfers · Shuttle

Bus · S-Bahn · Flugzeug · Taxi · Bahn/ICE
Bus · S-Bahn · Aeroplane · Taxi · Train/ICE

B3 Seminare und Konferenzen › Organisation
Seminars and conferences › Organisation

Fingerfood · Buffet · Business Lunch
Finger food · Buffet · Business Lunch

Kaffee · Tee · Plätzchen · Obst · Pause
Coffee · Tea · Biscuits · Fruit · Break

Anreise · Abreise
Arrival · Departure

Roter Teppich · Empfang
Red carpet · Reception

Garderobe
Cloakroom

B3 Seminare und Konferenzen / Seminars and conferences
› Programmpunkte / › Programme points

Vortrag · Impulsvortrag · Gastredner
Talk · Motivational talk · Guest speaker

Präsentation
Presentation

Podiumsdiskussion · Plenum · Forum
Podium discussion · Open to the floor · Forum

Pause
Break

B3 Seminare und Konferenzen / Seminars and conferences
› Programmpunkte / Programme points

Businesstheater · Improvisationstheater
Business theatre · Improvisational theatre

Wrap-Up · Rückblick · Zusammenfassung
Wrapping up · Review · Summary

Ehrung · Empfang · Auszeichnung · Jubiläum
Honour · Reception · Award · Celebration

Kamingespräch
Cosy chat

Seminare und Konferenzen / Seminars and conferences
› Rahmenprogramm
› Programme points

Menue à la Carte
A la cart menu

Gala-Dinner
Gala dinner

Abendprogramm · Band · Galashow
Evening programme · Band · Gala show

Come Together · Bargespräche
Get together · Bar meetings

Dresscode (casual · business casual · business · gala)
Dresscode (casual · business casual · business · gala)

Tanz · Musik · Party
Dance · Music · Party

C

Persönlichkeit, Team und Projekte

Personality, team and projects

C1 persönliche Entwicklung
Personal development

Die Höhen und Tiefen persönlicher Entwicklung sind für Einzelne wie auch für Gruppen und Teams ein immerwährendes Thema. Hier geht es vor allem um Stärken, Herausforderungen, besondere Fähigkeiten und Entwicklungspotentiale.

Diese und ähnliche Begriffe werden Ihnen vermutlich in Reflexionsphasen und tiefergehenden Teamdialogen begegnen. Nutzen Sie die folgenden Vorlagen, um beispielsweise eine Gruppe zu unterstützen oder sich einem schwierigen Thema zu nähern (z.B. zeigen Sie ein Bild und lassen die Gruppe darüber in den Dialog kommen).

Dokumentieren Sie einen wichtigen Diskurs der Gruppe, schreiben die Aussagen (O-Töne) mit und reichern diese mit Bildern an – auf diese Weise entsteht ein wichtiger Teil eines Bildprotokolls der gesamten Veranstaltung.

Oder Sie haben für ein Training einige Kernkompetenzen oder Herausforderungen im Fokus und visualisieren diese nun auf einzelnen Postern. So erhalten Sie eine visuelle Struktur, die Ihre Vorgehensweise unterstützt (roter Faden). Die Poster lassen sich ebenfalls für Themeninseln einsetzen.

Lassen Sie sich inspirieren, kombinieren Sie nach Herzenslust und entwickeln Sie Ihr visuelles Konzept, das Ihre Lernarchitektur, Ihre Vorgehensweise und/oder Ihr Setting optimal unterstützt.

The highs and lows of personal development are a perpetual theme for individuals and for groups and teams. Here, the main emphasis is on strengths, challenges, special skills and potential for development.

You have probably come across these and similar terms in reflective conversations and in-depth team dialogues. Use these templates to, for example, support a group to approach a difficult issue (e.g. show a picture and let the group get into dialogue about it). Document the major group discussion, write down statements (quotables) and enrich these with pictures – the result is an important part of a picture protocol for an entire event.

Or if you have a few key areas of expertise or challenges in mind for a training course, you can visualize them on individual posters. This gives you a visual structure to support your approach (main theme) or you can use the posters to design, for example, topic islands.

Let yourself be inspired, combine them to your heart's desire and develop your visual concept to provide optimum support for your learning architecture, your approach and/or your setting.

C1 persönliche Entwicklung / Personal development
› Persönlichkeit und Karriere / › Personality and career

Angriff · Offensive
Attack · Offensive

Verteidigung · Defensive
Defence · Defensive

Gegenwind
Head wind

Schutzengel · Intuition
Guardian angel · Intuition

Beruflicher Aufstieg · Karriere
Professional advancement · Career

C1 persönliche Entwicklung › Persönlichkeit und Karriere
Personal development › Personality and career

Fähigkeiten entecken
discover capabilities

Potentiale
Potential

Eigenliebe
Self-love

Angst zulassen
Admit fear

Angst loswerden
Get rid of fear

C1 persönliche Entwicklung › Persönlichkeit und Karriere
Personal development › Personality and career

Work-Life-Balance
Work-life balance

Überstunden
Overtime

Versicherung · Finanzielle Absicherung
Insurance · Financial security

Mobilität
Mobility

Multi-Tasking-Fähigkeit
Multitasking skills

C1 persönliche Entwicklung / Personal development
› Persönlichkeit und Karriere
› Personality and career

Selbstausdruck · Performance
Self-expression · Performance

über den Tellerrand schauen
Thinking outside the box

Offenheit · Lernbereitschaft
Openness · Willingness to learn

Selbsteinschätzung
Self-Assessment

Lernschritte · Lernstufen
Learning steps · Learning stages

C1 persönliche Entwicklung / Personal development
› Persönlichkeit und Karriere
› Personality and career

Wesensteile · Persönlichkeitsanteile · Kompetenzen
Aspects of character · Elements of personality · Capabilities

Selbstbild · positive/negative Anteile
Self-image · Positive/negative aspects

Reflexion · Selbstreflexion
Reflection · Self-reflection

Eigenverantwortung
Personal responsibility

Persönliches Wachstum · Entwicklung
Personal growth · Development

Coaching · Einzelcoaching
Coaching · Individual coaching

persönliche Entwicklung / Personal development
› Persönlichkeit und Karriere / › Personality and career

Motivierung
Motivation

Selbstmotivation · Motivation
Self-motivation · Motivation

Spezialist
Specialist

Ausbeutung
Exploitation

(Selbst-)Ausbeutung
(Self)exploitation

Generalist
Generalist

| C1 | **persönliche Entwicklung** ›Eigenschaften und Stärken
| | **Personal development** ›Characteristics and strengths

Ausdauer · Kondition
Stamina · Condition

Gelassenheit · Ruhe · Ausgeglichenheit
Composure · Calm · Harmony

Flexibilität
Flexibility

Power · Selbstbewusstsein
Power · Self-awareness

Selbstkontrolle · Balance · Risikobereitschaft
Self-control · Balance · Willingness to take risks

C1 persönliche Entwicklung / Personal development
› Eigenschaften und Stärken / Characteristics and strengths

Konzentration
Concentration

Kraft
Power

Schnelligkeit
Speed

Mut · Entschlossenheit
Courage · Decisiveness

Balance
Balance

| C1 persönliche Entwicklung | › Eigenschaften und Stärken |
| **Personal development** | › Characteristics and strengths |

Reaktionsvermögen
Reaction speed

Koordination
Coordination

Teamplay · Präzision
Team play · Precision

Aggression · Schmerztolleranz
Aggression · Pain threshold

Zielgenauigkeit
Accuracy

C2 Teamarbeit und Führung
Teamwork and leadership

Die im folgenden Kapitel visualisierten Themen und Begriffe stammen zum großen Teil von Konferenz- und Workshopteilnehmern. Es ist eine Sammlung zum Thema »Teamarbeit und Führung«, die vor allem Begriffe und Gedanken enthält, die uns mehr als einmal in unserer Arbeit begegnet sind. Wenn Sie häufig mit Themen rund um Kommunikation, Teamdynamik, Führung und Zusammenarbeit zu tun haben, dann finden Sie hier einige Bilder für Themen, die Ihnen in Ihrer Arbeit wahrscheinlich bereits begegnet sind.

Wenn Sie diese und ähnliche Visualisierungen live vor der Gruppe bzw. im Meeting, Workshop, etc. auf ein Plakat zeichnen (z.B. Flipchart), können Sie einzelne Aspekte enorm verstärken, um z.B. über einen Wert oder eine Anforderung zu reflektieren, um einen Aspekt zu betonen, um der Gruppe ein Feedback zu geben oder um sich auf eine Art der Zusammenarbeit zu verständigen.

TeilnehmerInnen identifizieren sich über lange Zeit hinweg mit den so entstandenen Dokumenten. Nutzen Sie die Kraft der Bilder und fördern Sie Verständigung und Verständnis durch das Gespräch über Bilder oder durch gemeinsames Visualisieren – gerade für tiefergehende Themen!

The subjects and terms visualized in the following chapter largely come from conference and workshop participants. It is a collection on the subject of «Teamwork and Management" which mainly contains terms and thoughts which we have come across more than once during our work. If you often deal with subjects relating to communications, team dynamics, management and cooperation, then this chapter includes some pictures for subjects you have probably already encountered during your work.

If you draw these visualizations on a poster live in front of a group or in a meeting, workshop, etc. (e.g. a flip chart), you can highlight individual aspects enormously in order to, for example, reflect on a value or a requirement, emphasise an aspect, give feedback to the group or make yourself clear about one form of cooperation.

Participants can identify with documents produced in this way for a long time. Utilise the power of images and promote communication and understanding by talking about pictures or through joint visualization – especially for more in-depth subjects!

C2 Teamarbeit und Führung › Dialog im Team
Teamwork and leadership › Team dialogue

miteinander reden
Talk to one another

Klartext reden · einfache Sprache benutzen
Talk in plain English · Use simple language

eine Sprache sprechen
Speaking one language

tun, was man sagt
walk the talk

wer A sagt muss auch B sagen
Whoever says A should also say B

wer muss informiert werden?
Who needs to be informed?

C2 Teamarbeit und Führung › Dialog im Team
Teamwork and leadership › Team dialogue

Dialog statt Beamer
Dialogue instead of projectors

etwas verständlich präsentieren · gut rüberbringen
Present things clearly · Convey things well

Raum für persönliche Gespräch schaffen
Create space for personal conversation

bereichsübergreifend arbeiten & kommunizieren
Work and communicate across departments

Informationstransfer
Information transfer

Gedanken, Vorurteile, Befürchtungen ansprechen
Address thoughts, prejudices, fears

C2 Teamarbeit und Führung › Teamdynamik
Teamwork and leadership › Team dynamic

Ablehnung · Ausgrenzung (schwarzes Schaf)
Rejection · Exclusion (black sheep)

Toleranz · Integration
Tolerance · Integration

Diversität · Unterschiedlichkeit
Diversity · Difference

Das Team fängt den einzelnen auf
The team collects the individuals

wir können uns nicht nur lieb haben
We cannot only love ourselves

Mobbing
Mobbing

C2 Teamarbeit und Führung › Führung
Teamwork and leadership › Leadership

Ansage · Führung · Entscheidungsmut
Announcement · Leadership · The courage to make decisions

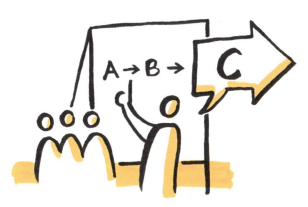

transparente Entscheidungen
Transparent decisions

eine Frage auf die nächste Ebene bringen
Escalating questions to the next level

Visionen realisieren · Strategien umsetzen
Turning visions into reality

die Leute mitnehmen
involve people

C2 Teamarbeit und Führung › Führung
Teamwork and leadership › Leadership

auf gleicher Augenhöhe
At the same eye-level

Rhetorik · welche Aussage zu welchem Zeitpunkt
Rhetoric · What statement at what point

Visionen versetzen Berge
Visions move mountains

gemeinsames Ziel
Common objective

Lösungsvorschläge statt Probleme liefern
Provide solutions instead of problems

Werte vorleben
Make examples of values

C2 Teamarbeit und Führung ›Zusammenarbeit
Teamwork and leadership ›Cooperation

Mauern einreissen
Tear down walls

Team als Basis für Erfolg
Team as basis for success

Führen · mit Leidenschaft führen
Leading · Leading with passion

Informationsflut
information flood

Rolle im Gesamtprozess
Role on process as a whole

gemeinsamer Aufstieg
Moving up together

› Zusammenarbeit
Teamwork and leadership › Cooperation

Gruppencoaching · Teamcoaching
Group coaching · Team coaching

Kooperation und Fleiß · reibungslose Abläufe
Cooperation and conscientiousness · Smooth processes

Mitarbeiter als Basis für Unternehmenserfolg
Employees as basis for company success

Team success · Dream team

Auftrieb · Ballast abwerfen
Impetus · Shed dead weight

Spiegelung · Spiegel vorhalten · Feedback
Reflection · Holding up a mirror · Feedback

C3 Projekte managen
Managing projects

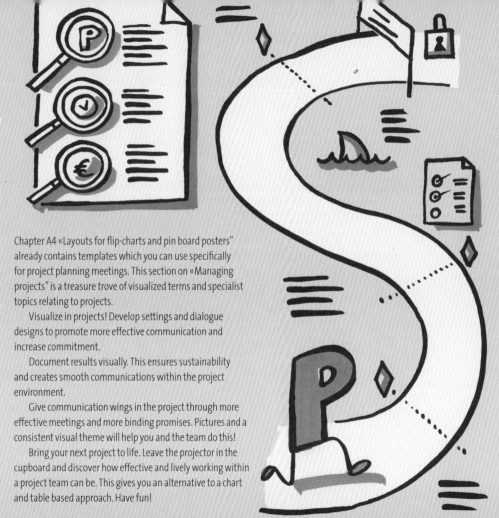

Im Kapitel A4 »Layouts für Flipcharts und Pinwandplakate« finden Sie bereits Vorlagen, die Sie speziell für Projektplanungsmeetings nutzen können. Der folgende Abschnitt »Projekte managen« ist eine Fundgrube visualisierter Begriffe und Spezialthemen rund um das Projekt.

Visualisieren Sie im Projekt! Entwickeln Sie Settings und Dialogarchitekturen, die effektivere Kommunikation fördern und die Verbindlichkeit erhöhen. Dokumentieren Sie Ergebnisse visuell. Dadurch sichern Sie die Nachhaltigkeit und sorgen im Projektumfeld für reibungslose Kommunikation.

Beflügeln Sie die Kommunikation im Projekt durch effektivere Meetings und verbindlichere Absprachen. Bilder und ein visueller, roter Faden helfen Ihnen und Ihrem Team dabei!

Bringen Sie Schwung in Ihr nächstes Projekt. Lassen Sie den Projektor im Schrank und machen Sie die Entdeckung, wie effektiv und lebendig Sie im Projektteam arbeiten können. Hiermit haben Sie eine Alternative zu matrix- und tabellengetriebenen Vorgehensweisen. Viel Spaß!

Chapter A4 «Layouts for flip-charts and pin board posters" already contains templates which you can use specifically for project planning meetings. This section on «Managing projects" is a treasure trove of visualized terms and specialist topics relating to projects.

Visualize in projects! Develop settings and dialogue designs to promote more effective communication and increase commitment.

Document results visually. This ensures sustainability and creates smooth communications within the project environment.

Give communication wings in the project through more effective meetings and more binding promises. Pictures and a consistent visual theme will help you and the team do this!

Bring your next project to life. Leave the projector in the cupboard and discover how effective and lively working within a project team can be. This gives you an alternative to a chart and table based approach. Have fun!

C3 Projekte managen
Managing projects

Projekt
Project

Projektmanagement
Project management

Projektbeschreibung & Hintergrund
Project description & background

Projektplanung
Project planning

abgeschlossenes Projekt
Completed project

Information
Information

Informationstausch
Information exchange

Informationsfluss
Information flow

C3 Projekte managen
Managing projects

Projekt-Status
Project status

Projektlebenszyklus
Project lifecycle

Projektmanagement-Standards
Project management standards

Projektmanagement · Projektmanager
Project management · Project manager

Zeitmanagement · Zeitmanager
Time management · Time manager

Budgetmanagement · Budgetmanager
Budget management · Budget manager

C3 Projekte managen
Managing projects

Meilenstein
Milestone

Projekt läuft
Project active

Projekt erreicht Meilenstein
Project achieved milestone

Projekt stagniert
Project stagnated

Projekt wird abgeschossen
Project concluded

Projekt erreicht Ziel
Project achieved target

Projekttiming
Project timing

Projektrisiken
Project risk

C3 Projekte managen / Managing projects

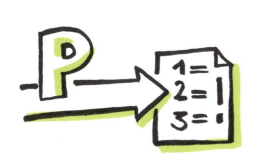

zu liefernde Ergebnisse (Deliverables)
Results to be achieved (Deliverables)

In Scope – Out of Scope
In Scope – Out of Scope

Plan B
Plan B

Restriktionen
Restrictions

Schnittstellen
Interfaces

Dokumentation
Documentation

C4 Informationstechnologie
Information technology

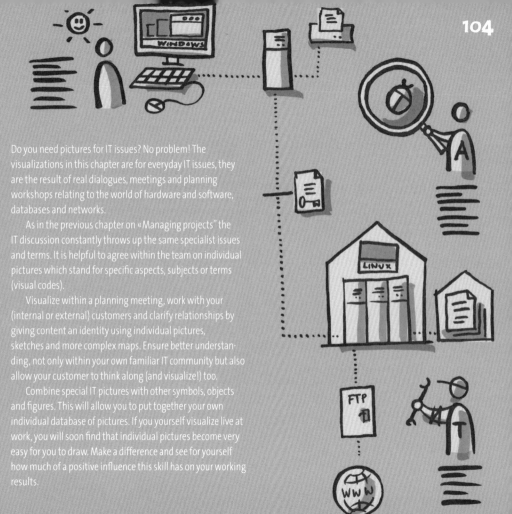

Benötigen Sie Bilder für IT-Themen? Bitteschön! Die im folgenden Kapitel zusammengestellten Visualisierungen sind IT-alltagstauglich, denn sie entspringen realen Dialogen, Meetings und Planungsworkshops rund um die Welt der Hard- und Software, der Datenbanken und Netzwerke.

Ähnlich wie im vorherigen Abschnitt »Projekte managen« werden Sie im IT-Diskurs spezielle Themen und Fachbegriffe verwenden, die immer wieder auftauchen. Es ist hilfreich, wenn Sie sich im Team auf einzelne Bilder verständigen, die für bestimmte Aspekte, Themen oder Begriffe stehen (visuelle Codes).

Visualisieren Sie im Planungsgespräch, beraten Sie Ihren (internen oder externen) Kunden und klären Sie Zusammenhänge, indem Sie Inhalten durch einzelne Bilder, Skizzen und komplexere Landkarten ein Gesicht geben. Sorgen Sie für ein besseres Verständnis nicht nur innerhalb Ihrer eingespielten IT-Gemeinde, sondern lassen Sie Ihren Kunden mitdenken (und mitvisualisieren!).

Kombinieren Sie spezielle IT-Bilder mit weiteren Symbolen, Gegenständen und Figuren und schon können Sie sich Ihre ganz individuelle Bilderdatenbank zusammenstellen. Wenn Sie in Ihrer Praxis selbst live visualisieren, werden Ihnen bald einzelne Bilder ganz locker von der Hand gehen. Machen Sie dadurch einen Unterschied und erleben Sie selbst, wie sehr diese Fähigkeit Ihre Arbeitsergebnisse positiv beeinflusst.

Do you need pictures for IT issues? No problem! The visualizations in this chapter are for everyday IT issues, they are the result of real dialogues, meetings and planning workshops relating to the world of hardware and software, databases and networks.

As in the previous chapter on «Managing projects" the IT discussion constantly throws up the same specialist issues and terms. It is helpful to agree within the team on individual pictures which stand for specific aspects, subjects or terms (visual codes).

Visualize within a planning meeting, work with your (internal or external) customers and clarify relationships by giving content an identity using individual pictures, sketches and more complex maps. Ensure better understanding, not only within your own familiar IT community but also allow your customer to think along (and visualize!) too.

Combine special IT pictures with other symbols, objects and figures. This will allow you to put together your own individual database of pictures. If you yourself visualize live at work, you will soon find that individual pictures become very easy for you to draw. Make a difference and see for yourself how much of a positive influence this skill has on your working results.

C4 Informationstechnologie › Hardware und Netzwerk
Information technology › Hardware and networks

Rechner · Personal Computer · PC
Computer · Personal Computer · PC

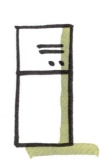

Laptop
Laptop

Server
Server

Server läuft · stürzt ab
Server running · crashes

Netzwerk · WLAN
Network · Wireless network

Drucker
Printer

Rechenzentrum
Computer centre

C4 Informationstechnologie › Software
Information technology › Software

106

Software (Programm)
Software (program)

Software-Entwicklung
Software development

Dokument
Document

E-Mail
E-mail

Datenbank
Database

(FTP-)Zugang
(FTP) access

Internet · World Wide Web
Internet · World Wide Web

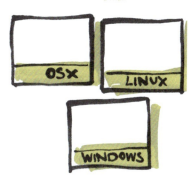

Betriebssystem
Operating system

C4 Informationstechnologie / Information technology
› weitere IT-Begriffe
› Other IT terms

Netzwerktechniker
Network technician

Administrator
Administrator

User
User

Protokoll
protocol

Passwort
Password

geschützte Datei
Protected file

Bug (Programmierfehler) · Fehler-Report · Fehlersuche
Bug (programming error) · Error report · Troubleshooting

D

Unternehmen und Markt
Company and market

D1 Unternehmen/Organisation
Company/Organisation

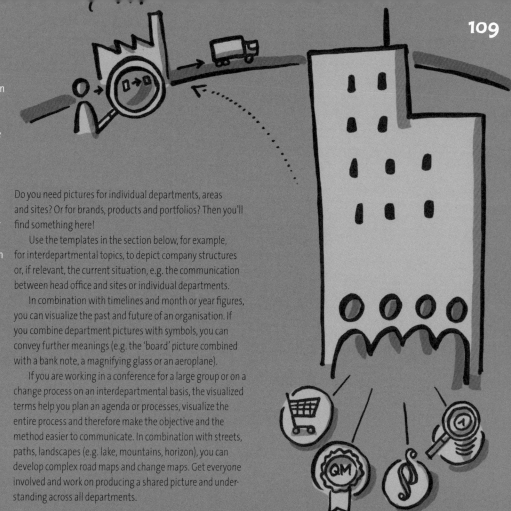

Benötigen Sie Bilder für einzelne Abteilungen, Bereiche und Standorte? Geht es um Marken, Produkte und Portfolios? Dann werden Sie hier fündig!

Verwenden Sie die im folgenden Abschnitt zusammengestellten Vorlagen zum Beispiel für abteilungsübergreifende Themen, für die Darstellung von Unternehmensstrukturen oder wenn es darum geht, eine Ist-Situation, zum Beispiel die Kommunikation zwischen der Zentrale und Standorten sowie einzelnen Abteilungen, zu thematisieren.

In Kombination mit Zeitleisten und Monats- oder Jahreszahlen können Sie die Vergangenheit und Zukunft einer Organisation visualisieren. Wenn Sie die Abteilungsbilder mit Symbolen kombinieren, erhalten Sie weitere Bedeutungen (z.B. Bild »Vorstand« kombiniert mit einem Geldschein, einer Lupe oder einem Flugzeug).

Wenn Sie in einer Großgruppenkonferenz oder einem Veränderungsprozess abteilungsübergreifend arbeiten, helfen Ihnen die visualisierten Begriffe, eine Agenda oder Abläufe zu planen, den gesamten Prozess zu visualisieren und dadurch Ziel und Weg leichter zu vermitteln. In Kombination mit Straßen, Wegen, Landschaften (z.B. See, Berge, Horizont) entwickeln Sie komplexe Roadmaps und Change-Landkarten. Sorgen Sie für Beteiligung und arbeiten Sie bereichsübergreifend an einem gemeinsamen Bild und Verständnis.

Do you need pictures for individual departments, areas and sites? Or for brands, products and portfolios? Then you'll find something here!

Use the templates in the section below, for example, for interdepartmental topics, to depict company structures or, if relevant, the current situation, e.g. the communication between head office and sites or individual departments.

In combination with timelines and month or year figures, you can visualize the past and future of an organisation. If you combine department pictures with symbols, you can convey further meanings (e.g. the 'board' picture combined with a bank note, a magnifying glass or an aeroplane).

If you are working in a conference for a large group or on a change process on an interdepartmental basis, the visualized terms help you plan an agenda or processes, visualize the entire process and therefore make the objective and the method easier to communicate. In combination with streets, paths, landscapes (e.g. lake, mountains, horizon), you can develop complex road maps and change maps. Get everyone involved and work on producing a shared picture and understanding across all departments.

| **D1** | **Unternehmen** | › Unternehmensstruktur |
| | **Company** | › Company structure |

Unternehmen
Company

Betrieb · Produktion
Works · Production

Vorstand
Board

Aufsichtsrat
Supervisory board

Geschäftsführung
Management

Inhaber
Owner

Anteilseigner
Shareholder

Bereich · Abteilung
Division · Department

D1 Unternehmen / Company
› Abteilungen
› Departments

Betriebsrat
Works council

Change Management
Change Management

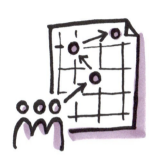

Organisationsentwicklung
Organisational development

Strategie
Strategy

Einkauf
Purchasing

Verkauf · Vertrieb
Sales · Distribution

Marketing · Public Relations · Werbung
Marketing · Public relations · Advertising

IT
IT

D1 Unternehmen / Company
› Abteilungen / Departments

Personal · Personalentwicklung
Personnel · Personnel development

Forschung und Entwicklung
Research and development

Interne Kommunikation
Internal communication

Qualitätsmanagement
Quality Management

Logistik · Transport
Logistics · Transport

Finanzen
Finances

Controlling
Controlling

Recht
Law

D1 Unternehmen / Company
› Abteilungen / Departments

Innendienst · Außendienst
Internal sales · External sales

Unternehmenskommunikation
Corporate communication

Telefonzentrale
Telephone centre

Callcenter
Call centre

Sekretariat · Administration
Secretary · Administration

Gebäude- / Facility-Management
Building / Facility Management

Supply Chain Management
Supply Chain Management

Versand · Lager
Shipping · Warehouse

D1 Unternehmen / Company
› Unternehmensbegriffe
› Company terms

Produkt
Product

Marke
Brand

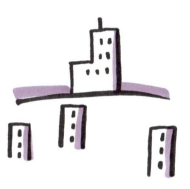
Zentrale und Niederlassungen
Head office and branches

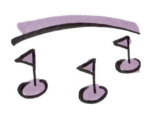
Standorte
Locations

Lieferanten · Zulieferer
Suppliers · Providers

Portfolio
Portfolio

Direktvertrieb
Direct sales

D2 Strategie, Kunde und Markt
Strategy, customer and market

Strategieumsetzung, Umstrukturierung, interne Prozesse und Zusammenarbeit spielen in strategischen Dialogen ebenso eine Rolle wie Themen des Umfelds wie etwa Rahmenbedingungen der Volkswirtschaft und Kunden- und Wettbewerberverhalten. Zu diesen und weiteren Themen im Spannungsfeld »Strategie, Kunde und Markt« liefert dieser Abschnitt visuelle Umsetzungen.

Hier finden sich vor allem kompexere Bilder, die durch die Kombination verschiedener Symbole zum Teil sehr konkrete Themen und Sachverhalte darstellen. Nutzen Sie diese Sammlung z. B. zur visuellen Begleitung entsprechender Dialoge in Meetings, Tagungen und Konferenzen (z.B. Live-Visualisierung auf Wandzeitung). Gestalten Sie eigene Plakate und Vorlagen für Gruppenarbeiten oder lassen Sie sich einfach von den verschiedenen Bildern und der Kombination visueller Codes inspirieren (z. B. Haifischflosse im Meer, Münzen und Figuren). Entdecken Sie durch eigene, neue Kombinationen (auch Wort-Bild-Kombinationen!) neue Bedeutungen. Helfen Sie damit KollegInnen und Führungskräften in strategischen Dialogen durchzublicken und – vor allem – über die gleiche Sache (das gleiche Bild) zu sprechen.

Ein treffendes Bild zur richtigen Zeit wirkt Wunder: Bringen Sie es auf den Punkt. Entwickeln Sie eine gemeinsame Sichtweise. Nutzen Sie Bilder, wenn es darum geht, Strategien zu entwickeln und zu kommunizieren!

In strategic dialogues, strategy implementation, restructuring, internal processes and cooperation play as important a role as issues surrounding the environment, such as the framework economic conditions and customer and competitor behaviour. This section provides visual interpretations of common issues and terms for these and other issues in the exciting field of «strategy, customer and market".

The main focus here is on more complex pictures which sometimes represent concrete issues and content by combining different symbols. Use this collection, for example, as a visual accompaniment to relevant dialogues in meetings and conferences (e.g. live visualization on a wall newspaper), design your own posters and templates for group work or simply take inspiration from the different pictures and the combination of visual codes (e.g. shark fin in the see, coins and figures). Use your own new combinations (including combinations of pictures and words) to discover new meanings. Help colleagues and management understand in strategic dialogues and – most importantly – talk about the same thing (the same picture).

An appropriate picture at the right time works wonders: Get to the point. Develop a shared perspective. Use pictures to develop strategies and communicate!

D2 Strategie, Kunde und Markt / Strategy, customer and market
› Strategie / › Strategy

Strategie · Schlachtplan
Strategy · Plan of attack

das ganze Bild sehen
Seeing the whole picture

Strategien umsetzen · Roll out · Implementierung
Implementing strategies · Rollout · Implementation

an einem Strang ziehen
Pulling together

Change · Umstrukturierung · Reengineering
Change · Restructuring · Reengineering

Globales Portfolio
Global portfolio

D2 Strategie, Kunde und Markt — › Strategie
Strategy, customer and market — › Strategy

Win-Win Situation
Win-win situation

Offshoring
Offshoring

Cash Cow
Cash Cow

Firmenumzug · Standortverlegung
Company relocation · Change of site

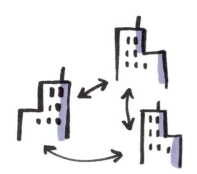

Vernetzung
Networking

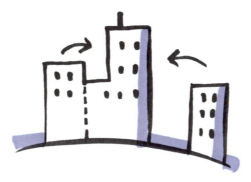

Fusion · Merger
Fusion · Merger

Akquisition
Acquisition

D2 Strategie, Kunde und Markt / Strategy, customer and market
› Kunde und Markt / Customer and market

Leistungsportfolio verstehen
Understanding the service portfolio

Kunde als König
Customer as king

Kunde als Partner
Customer as partner

Was bringt's dem Kunden?
What's in it for the customer?

interner Kunde
Internal customer

Kundengewinnung
Customer acquisition

Geschäftskunde
Business to Business

Endkunde
Business to Customer

D2 Strategie, Kunde und Markt / Strategy, customer and market
› Kunde und Markt
› Customer and market

eine Anlaufstelle für den Kunden
One face to the customer

vom Problem zur Geschäfts-Möglichkeit
Turning a problem into a business opportunity

Servicequalität
Service quality

die Schnellen schlagen die Großen
Speed overcomes size

aus einem Geschäft/Markt mehr rausholen
Getting more out of a business/market

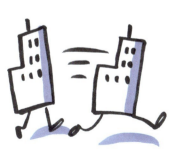

schneller sein als der Wettbewerb
Being quicker than the competition

Regionaler Markt
Regional market

Marktbeobachtung · Marktanalyse
Market observation · Market analysis

D2 Strategie, Kunde und Markt / Strategy, customer and market
› interne Prozesse
› Internal processes

zu viel Verwaltungs-Aufgaben · Administration
Too much administration work · Administration

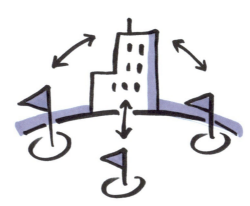

Zusammenspiel zwischen Zentrale & Fläche
Interaction between head office and lower levels

Muster aufbrechen
Breaking down pattern

Prozessoptimierung · Produktionsoptimierung
Process optimisation · Production optimisation

Dem Geld hinterher rennen
Chasing money

transparente Strukturen · Schnittstellen · Zuständigkeiten
Transparent structures · Interfaces · Responsibilities

D2 Strategie, Kunde und Markt
Strategy, customer and market

› interne Prozesse
› Internal processes

Erfolge messen · Benchmarking
Measuring success · Benchmarking

Was steckt unter der Oberfläche?
What is beneath the surface?

Einheitsgröße!?
One size fits all!?

Meilenstein überwinden
Overcoming milestone

Startphase
Kick-off

Werkzeuge
Tools

D2 Strategie, Kunde und Markt / Strategy, customer and market

› Unternehmenskultur
› Internal processes

Geschäftserfolg durch gelebte Werte
Business success by living values

Wertschätzung von Vielfalt
Cultural Diversity

weltweite Einheit · eine Identität
Global unit · One identity

Globales Meeting · Internationales Business
Global meeting · International business

Ideenmanagement · Vorschlagswesen
Ideas management · Suggestion system

global denken, lokal handeln
Think global, act local

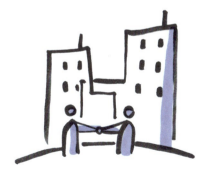

Firmenkulturen verschmelzen · Fusion
Merging company cultures · Fusion

D2	Strategie, Kunde und Markt	› Finanzwirtschaft
	Strategy, customer and market	› Financial system

Bank · Börse
Bank · Stock market

Börsenboom · Börsencrash
Stock market boom · Stock market crash

Finanzkrise
Financial crisis

Konjunktur
Economic trend

Aufschwung · Abschwung
Upturn · Downturn

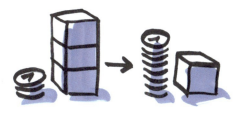

Inflation
Inflation

D2 Strategie, Kunde und Markt / Strategy, customer and market
› Volkswirtschaft
› Economy

Wirtschaftskrise
Economic crisis

Entwicklung
Development

Nachhaltigkeit
Sustainability

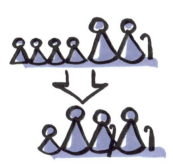

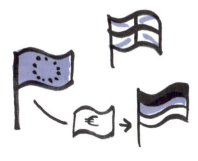

Globalisierung · Internationalisierung
Globalisation · Internationalisation

demografischer Wandel
Demographic change

EU · Staaten · Subventionen
EU countries · Subsidies

Anhang
Appendix

Literature recommendations

Scholz, Holger (2008) Lernlandkarte Nr. 4 – Visual Facilitating & Graphic Recording. Eichenzell: Neuland GmbH & Co.KG & Kommunikationslotsen. Internationale Bestelladressen: www.neuland.com
ISBN 978-3-940315-04-5

Sibbet, David. The Grove Consultants International (2006) Graphic Facilitation: Transforming Group Process with the Power of Visual Listening. Facilitation Guide Series, Shop: http://store.grove.com/

Margulies, Nancy & Maal, Nusa (2002) Mapping Inner Space: Learning and Teaching Visual Mapping. Tucson: Zephyr Press. ISBN 1-56976-138-8. 2. Auflage: 2Rev Ed (2004) Crown House Publishing. ISBN-10: 1904424473, ISBN-13: 978-1904424475

Roam, Dan (2008) The Back of the Napkin: Solving Problems and Selling Ideas with Pictures. New York: Penguin Group. ISBN 978-1-59184-199-9

Horn, Robert E. (1998) Visual Language: Global Communication for the 21st Century. MacroVU Press. ISBN-10: 189263709X, ISBN-13: 978-1892637093

Scholz, Holger (2008) Learning map No. 4 – Visual Facilitating & Graphic Recording. Eichenzell: Neuland GmbH & Co.KG & Kommunikationslotsen. International ordering addresses: www.neuland.com
ISBN 978-3-940315-04-5

Sibbet, David. The Grove Consultants International (2006) Graphic Facilitation: Transforming Group Process with the Power of Visual Listening. Facilitation Guide Series, Shop: http://store.grove.com/

Margulies, Nancy & Maal, Nusa (2002) Mapping Inner Space: Learning and Teaching Visual Mapping. Tucson: Zephyr Press. ISBN 1-56976-138-8. 2. Auflage: 2Rev Ed (2004) Crown House Publishing. ISBN-10: 1904424473, ISBN-13: 978-1904424475

Roam, Dan (2008) The Back of the Napkin: Solving Problems and Selling Ideas with Pictures. New York: Penguin Group. ISBN 978-1-59184-199-9

Horn, Robert E. (1998) Visual Language: Global Communication for the 21st Century. MacroVU Press. ISBN-10: 189263709X, ISBN-13: 978-1892637093

Web recommendations

bikablo® akademie further training:
www.bikablo.com

Colleagues:
- Brandy Agerbeck: www.loosetooth.com
- Reinhard Kuchenmüller: www.visuelle-protokolle.de
- Ursula Arztmann: www.innovation-factory.ch
- Dan Roam, author of «The Back of the Napkin": www.thebackofthenapkin.com
- Christina Merkley, who combines coaching with visualization: http://www.shift-it-coach.com/portfolio/
- Stephanie Crowley, Graphic Recorder: www.TheChrysalisSolution.com
  ... and a video on YouTube about her work: www.youtube.com/user/ChrysalisStudios
- David Sibbet, the Visual Facilitating pioneer from the USA: www.grove.com

Forums and Organisations:
- IFVP (International Forum of Visual Practitioners): www.ifvpcommunity.ning.com/
- Visual Thinking Association in the USA, which also organises conferences in Europe: www.vizthink.com
- WorldwideForum for Graphic Facilitation and its marginal areas: www.graphicfacilitation.com

Visualization and coloration with Neuland Outliner and BigOnes

- **Verwenden Sie für die Konturlinie den wischfesten und nicht durchschlagenden Neuland Outliner.** So erreichen Sie eine ruhige, einheitliche Gesamtwirkung und bleiben flexibel in der späteren Farbgebung.
- **Verwenden Sie zum Colorieren und Schattieren (s. S. 5) helle Farbtöne der BigOnes.** Die dunklen Farben des Sortiments wie blau, violett, dunkelbraun oder dunkelrot eignen sich weniger dafür.
- **Verwenden Sie nicht zu viele unterschiedliche Farben** für eine Visualisierung. Wählen Sie die Farben nach folgenden Kriterien aus:
  > **Farbtöne aus einem Bereich** (z. B. Pastelltöne ODER Erdtöne)
  > **benachbarte Farbtöne**, z. B. orange/gelb/brillantgelb/pastellgelb; hellgrün/türkis/hellblau/pastellblau; rosa/pink/pastellviolett
- **grau** passt zu jeder Farbe!

- **Use the smudge-proof and non-penetrating Neuland Outliner for the contour line.** This allows you to achieve a smooth, unified overall impression and remains flexible when adding color later.
- **Use the light BigOnes colors for coloring and shading (see p.5).** The dark colors in the range such as blue, violet, dark brown or dark red are less suitable for this purpose.
- **Do not use too many different colors for a visualization.** Select a color using the following criteria:
  > **Colors from one sector** (e.g. pastels OR earth tones)
  > **Neighbouring colors,** e.g. orange/yellow/brilliant yellow/pastel yellow; light green/turquoise/ light blue/pastel blue; rose/pink/pastel violet
- **grey** goes with any color!

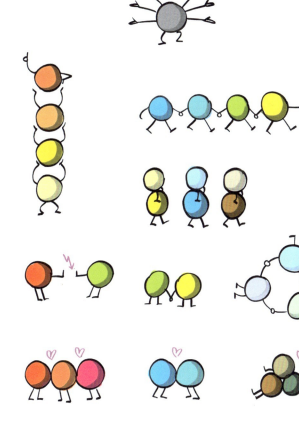

Das Praxisbuch zur bikablo®-Visualisierungstechnik
U, Z, M und O bilden die kleine Glühbirne, die inspiriert und neue Gedanken aus Köpfen und Herzen lockt. Bikablo®-Erfinder Martin Haussmann stellt erstmalig ein Gesamtsystem aus visuellem Lernen, Sketchnoting, Graphic Recording und Visual Facilitating vor. Für dieses Buch wurde der Redline-Verlag als Partner gewonnen, um auch Menschen außerhalb des Neuland-Universums für visuelles Denken zu begeistern. Als Mitglied der »bikablo®-Familie« ist das Buch natürlich bei Neuland erhältlich. 304 Seiten, durchgehend vierfarbig. ISBN 978-3-86881-517-7

(nur auf deutsch – only in German)

bikablo® products

b bikablo® 1

Visuelles Wörterbuch
Der »Ur-bikablo®« (Bilder-Karten-Block) ist Ihre Eintrittskarte in die Welt der Visualisierung: Ein einzigartiges Nachschlagewerk der Bildsprache mit hunderten von erfolgreichen Bildsymbolen auf 133 Seiten in der einfach zu zeichnenden bikablo®-Technik.
ISBN 978-3-940315-21-2

Visual Dictionary
The 'first bikablo®' (image card block) is your admission ticket to the world of visualization: a unique reference work of visual communication with hundreds of successful visual symbols on 133 pages using the easy-to-draw bikablo® technique. ISBN 978-3-940315-21-2

b bikablo® emotions

Visuelles Wörterbuch
Kleine Figuren mit großen Gefühlen! Mit zwei neuen, einfach abzuzeichnenden Figurentypen präsentiert bikablo® emotions den Menschen, seine Gefühle und seine Interaktion mit anderen – von A wie »aufgedreht« bis Z wie »zufrieden«. ISBN 978-3940315-16-8

Visual Dictionary
Small figures with big emotions! bikablo® emotions presents two new, simple to copy figure types of people to show emotions and interaction with others – from A for 'amazed' to Z for 'zealous'. ISBN 978-3940315-16-8

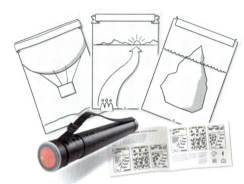

b bikablo® posters

FlipChart-Vorlagen für Visualisierung
Die 10 erfolgreichsten FlipChart-Plakatvorlagen zum reinschreiben, durchpausen oder mit mitgelieferter Transparentfolie und Whiteboard-Marker immer wieder neu beschriften. Mit ausführlichem Methoden-Beiheft und vielen Anwendungsbeispielen.

Flipchart Templates for Visualization
The 10 most successful flipchart poster templates to write on, trace or overwrite with the included transparent foil and whiteboard markers. Includes detailed supplementary booklet and many example applications.

 bikablo® **icons**

Kartenbox für visuelle Methoden
120 Symbole, 30 Aktions- und 60 Emotionskarten in der praktischen Novario®-Box: Noch nie war es so einfach, mit den beliebten bikablo®-Motiven Ihre Visualisierung zu bereichern! Incl. ausführlichem Beiheft, leeren Karten und 3 Markern. ISBN 978-3940315-15-1

Card Box for Visual Methods
120 symbols, 30 action and 60 emotion cards in the practical Novario® box: it has never been easier to enrich your visualization using the popular bikablo® motifs! Includes detailed supplementary booklet, empty cards and 3 marker. ISBN 978-3940315-15-1

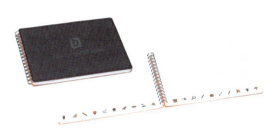

 bikablo® **sketchbook**

Skizzenbuch mit visuellen Vorlagen und Übungen
Ein Skizzenbuch mit inspirierendem »Symbol-Spickzettel« und einfachen Visualisierungsaufgaben, die in die Grundlogik der bikablo® Zeichentechnik einführen. Zum Visualisieren üben, Ideen notieren oder einfach nur reinkritzeln.

Sketchbook with Visual Templates and Exercises
A sketchbook with an inspiring 'symbol cheat sheet' and simple visualization tasks to introduce you to the basic logic behind bikablo® drawing techniques. For you to practise visualization, note down ideas or just doodle.

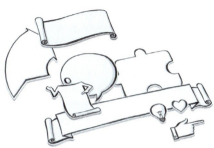

bikablo® **workshop cards**

Ideencontainer für die Pinwand
Die Ausdruckskraft der Visualisierung im eigenen Training anwenden: vorgestanzte Formen und »Textcontainer« für die Pinwand und viele weitere Einsatzmöglichkeiten rund um Trainings, Workshops, Meetings und Konferenzen.

Idea Containier for Pinboard
Use the expressive nature of visualization in your own training sessions: pre-cut forms and 'text container' for the pinboard and many other possible uses.

Lernlandkarten
Learning Maps

facilitating tools by kommunikationslotsen

Lernlandkarte Nr. 1 – Open Space
Sie wollten schon immer wissen, was Open Space nun eigentlich genau ist – hier erhalten Sie einem umfassenden Einblick.
ISBN 978-3-940315-01-4

Lernlandkarte Nr. 2 – World Café
Das Verfahren, das einen maximalen Dialog und intensive Gespräche in angenehmer Atmosphäre, z.B. in Workshops und Konferenzen, ermöglicht. ISBN 978-3-940315-02-1

Lernlandkarte Nr. 3 – Appreciative Inquiry
Darin finden Sie alles Wichtige über die erfolgreiche Alternative zu herkömmlichen Problemlösungs-Strategien.
ISBN 978-3-940315-03-8

Lernlandkarte Nr. 4 – Visual Facilitating & Graphic Recording
In dieser Lernlandkarte finden Sie alles Wichtige für einen Einstieg in die Welt der Visualisierung und visuellen Moderation. ISBN 978-3-940315-04-5

Lernlandkarte Nr. 5 – Storytelling
Alles Wichtige, um sich mit einem wirkungsvollen Werkzeug für Führungskräfte und Facilitatoren vertraut zu machen – der Kunst des Geschichtenerzählens.
ISBN 978-3-940315-06-9

Lernlandkarte Nr. 6 – Projektmanagement
Alles Wichtige, um sich mit den Grundzügen des Projektmanagements bekannt zu machen. ISBN 978-3-940315-07-6

Lernlandkarte Nr. 7 – Zukunftskonferenz
Eine kompakte Einführung in eine komplexe Methode, mit der es gelingt, in einem ganzen System Zukunft zu gestalten.
ISBN 978-3-940315-08-3

Lernlandkarte Nr. 8 – Dynamic Facilitation
Alles Wichtige, um Sie mit einer Methode bekannt zu machen, die scheinbar unlösbare Probleme und vertrackte Dilemmata in Gruppen transformiert. ISBN 978-3-940315-18-2

Lernlandkarte Nr. 9 – The Circle Way
Eine Dialogmethode, die interkulturell eingesetzt werden kann. Kreisarbeit bedeutet Präsenz, Verantwortlichkeit und effiziente Führung. ISBN 978-3-940315-20-5

Learning map No. 1 – Open Space
If you always wanted to know exactly what Open Space is and you are looking for a comprehensive guide. ISBN 978-3-940315-01-4

Learning map No. 2 – World Café
The process which allows maximum dialogue and intensive conversation within a pleasant atmosphere, e.g. in workshops and conferences. ISBN 978-3-940315-02-1

Learning map No. 3 – Appreciative Inquiry
All the important information on the successful alternative to conventional problem solving strategies.
ISBN 978-3-940315-03-8

Learning map No. 4 – Visual Facilitating & Graphic Recording
This leaning map contains all the important information for entering into the world of visualization and visual moderation.
ISBN 978-3-940315-04-5

Learning map No. 5 – Storytelling
All the important information you need to get familiar with an effective tool for management and facilitators – the art of storytelling. ISBN 978-3-940315-06-9

Learning map No. 6 – Project Management
This learning map includes everything you need to understand the basics of project management. ISBN 978-3-940315-07-6

Learning map No. 7 – Future Search
A dense introduction to a complex method for designing the future in a whole system.
ISBN 978-3-940315-08-3

Learning map No. 8 – Dynamic Facilitation
All the important information you need to get familiar with a method that transforms apparently insolvable problems and dodgy dilemmata in groups. ISBN 978-3-940315-18-2

Learning map No. 9 – The Circle Way
A conversational methodology which can be used cross-culturally. Circle is about presence, accountability and effective leadership.
ISBN 978-3-940315-20-5

Method sets

World Café Material
Mit der Dialogmethode World Café schaffen Sie Raum für echte Begegnung und Austausch. Wir unterstützen Sie dabei mit dem Tischaufsteller World Café-Etikette und Tischdecken zum Draufschreiben in unterschiedlichen Formaten.

World Café Material
The World Café dialog method creates space for real meeting and exchange. We provide support with the table displays with the World Café stickers and tablecloths to write on in various formats.

Open Space Material
Dieses Set versorgt Sie mit dem wichtigsten Basis- Know-how und Material für die Durchführung eines Open Space mit bis zu 120 Teilnehmern: Lernlandkarte Open Space, Prinzipien- und Ergebnisplakate, Karten und Marker.

Open Space Material
This set supplies you with the most important basic know-how and materials to carry out an Open Space with up to 120 participants: Open Space learning map, principle and result posters, cards and markers.

Internationale Bestelladressen • **International ordering addresses:** www.neuland.com

Further training — bikablo® akademie

In unseren **bikablo® Visualisierungstrainings** bieten wir Ihnen den Einstieg in die wunderbare Welt der visuellen Sprache. Sie starten von Ihrem individuellen Stand aus und lernen an 2 Tagen **Visualisieren mit der bikablo® Technik,** einer einfach zu lernenden, systematischen visuellen Sprache, auf der auch unsere bikablo® Produkte basieren.

Im **Visual Facilitator Curriculum** bieten wir Visual Facilitating für Fortgeschrittene an: Visual Storytelling, Graphic Recording, Visual Meeting Facilitation und Visual Consulting. Die **Trainings-Specials** decken darüber hinaus spezielle Themen ab – von Sketchnoting bis Visual Scrum. Unsere **Visualisierungstrainings inhouse** werden maßgeschneidert auf die Bedürfnisse Ihrer Firma, Ihres Verbands oder Netzwerks. Wenn Sie sich für Methodenwissen, Moderations-Verfahren und Fragen der Prozessbegleitung (Facilitation) interessieren, empfehlen wir Ihnen das **Facilitator Curriculum** der Kommunikationslotsen.

Our **bikablo® Visualization Training Sessions** offer you an introduction into the wonderful world of visual language. Begin at your personal starting point and spend 2 days learning **Visualization with the bikablo® technique,** the easy-to-learn, systematic visual language on which our bikablo® products are also based.

The **Visual Facilitator Curriculum** offers Visual Facilitating for the more advanced: Visual Storytelling, Graphic Recording, Visual Meeting Facilitation and Visual Consulting. The **training specials** cover special topics like Sketchnoting or Visual Scrum. Our **Visual Facilitating In-house Training Sessions** are tailored to the needs of your company, your association or network. If you are interested in methodological expertise, presentation procedures and questions of facilitation then we recommend the **Facilitator Curriculum** of Kommunikationslotsen.

Termine, Infos und Anmeldung • Dates, information and registration:
www.bikablo.com

The authors, credits

bikablo® 2.0
Visuelles Wörterbuch
neue Bilder für Training,
Meeting und Learning

bikablo® 2.0
Visual Vocabulary
new Visuals for Training,
Meeting and Learning

www.bikablo.com

Text: Holger Scholz und Martin Haussmann
Gestaltung und Illustrationen: Martin Haussmann
Mitarbeit: Ceren Haussmann
unter Verwendung von Bildideen von: Karina Antons, Ceren Haussmann, Kirsten Reinhold

Holger Scholz, *1968, ist Gründer und Gesellschafter der Unternehmensberatung Kommunikationslotsen. Er arbeitet als Facilitator und Consultant (IAF Certified Professional Facilitator) sowie als Trainer zu den Themen Facilitation und Leadership.

Martin Haussmann, *1969, studierte Visuelle Kommunikation in Stuttgart und Illustration in Wuppertal. Seit 1995 arbeitet er als freischaffender Designer und Illustrator in Köln, seit 2003 ist er assoziierter Partner der Kommunikationslotsen und seit 2015 Geschäftsführer der bikablo® akademie.

Text: Holger Scholz and Martin Haussmann
Design and illustrations: Martin Haussmann
Collaboration: Ceren Haussmann
Using visual ideas by: Karina Antons, Ceren Haussmann, Kirsten Reinhold

Holger Scholz, born in 1968, is a founder and shareholder of management consultancy company Kommunikationslotsen. He works as a facilitator and consultant (IAF Certified Professional Facilitator) and as a trainer on facilitation and leadership.

Martin Haussmann, born in 1969, studied Visual Communication at Stuttgart and Illustration at Wuppertal. Since 1995, he has been working as a freelance designer and illustrator in Cologne, joined Kommunikationslotsen as an associate partner in 2003 and is the managing director of the bikablo® akademie since 2015.

Urheberrechtliche Hinweise: Die Illustrationen im bikablo® 2.0 sind urheberrechtlich geschützt. Sie dürfen sie abzeichnen und so für Ihre Arbeit verwenden. Es ist untersagt, die Illustrationen fotomechanisch oder digital zu reproduzieren und in gedruckten oder digitalen Publikationen (Broschüren, Büchern, Internet etc.) zu verwenden.

Vertrieb: Distribution:
Neuland GmbH & Co. KG
Am Kreuzacker 7
D 36124 Eichenzell / Germany
Fon: +49 (0) 66 59 – 88-100
Fax: +49 (0) 66 59 – 88-188
info@neuland.com

Internationale Bestelladressen:
international ordering addresses:
www.neuland.com

Copyright notice: The illustrations in bikablo® 2.0 are protected by copyright. You can copy them and use them for your work. However, the illustrations may not be photographically or digitally reproduced and used elsewhere in printed or digital publications (brochures, books, internet, etc.).

bikablo® akademie

Herausgeber: Editor:
bikablo® akademie GmbH & Co. KG
ein Unternehmen der Kommunikationslotsen
a Kommunikationslotsen company
Lüderichstr. 2–4, D-51105 Köln
Tel: +49 (0)221. 98 93 68 64
info@bikablo.com
www.bikablo.com
www.kommunikationslotsen.de

9. Auflage © Haussmann / Scholz, bikablo® akademie 2016